DAVID BOWIE
CHANGES

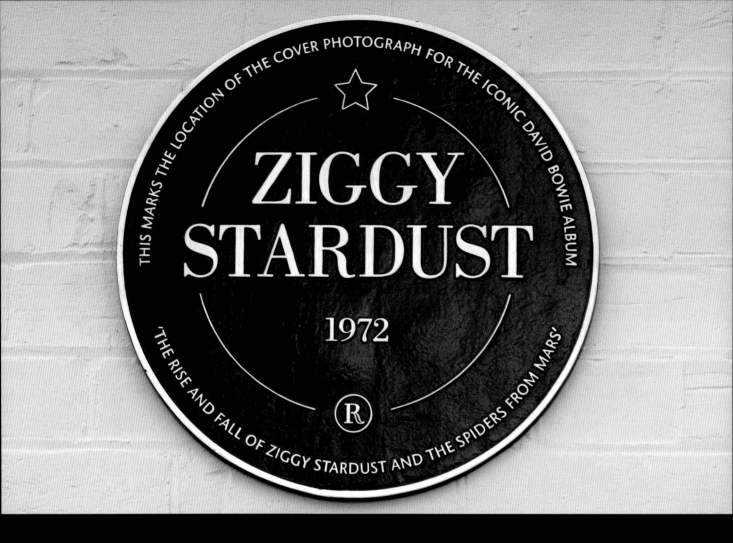

THIS MARKS THE LOCATION OF THE COVER PHOTOGRAPH FOR THE ICONIC DAVID BOWIE ALBUM

ZIGGY STARDUST

1972

'THE RISE AND FALL OF ZIGGY STARDUST AND THE SPIDERS FROM MARS'

THIS IS A CARLTON BOOK

This edition published in 2016

First published in 2013 by Carlton Books
An imprint of the Carlton Publishing Group
20 Mortimer Street

DAVID BOWIE
CHANGES

CHRIS WELCH

CARLTON
BOOKS

THE EARLY YEARS

MAJOR TOM

THE RISE AND FALL OF ZIGGY STARDUST

UNLEASH THE DIAMOND DOGS

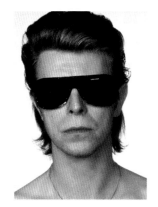

INTRODUCTION

David Byrne of Talking Heads, asked to sum up the essence of David Bowie once proclaimed amidst much hyperbole that he was a "shrink, priest, sex object and prophet of doom." Woody Woodmansey, a true Spider from Mars, when asked the same question replied with a single word: "Genius".

Byrne was speaking at the 1996 Rock and Roll Hall of Fame induction ceremony in New York, USA when luminaries of the music industry gathered to pay tribute to a towering giant of popular music. Woodmansey however was addressing a small gathering of devoted fans at a 2012 'Bowie fest' in England.

Held at London's ICA Gallery the event celebrated the 40th anniversary of the release of seminal album *The Rise and Fall of Ziggy Stardust and the Spiders From Mars*. Both men, from their different perspectives, emphasized the enormous impact Bowie had made on them and the world at large, during an extraordinary career when his artistic output encompassed music, film, fashion and theatre.

Byrne, himself an influential composer and performer, explained how Bowie had provided rock 'n' roll with "a shot in the arm." David's abrupt appearance in early Seventies' America with such albums as *The Man Who Sold The World*, *Hunky Dory* and *Aladdin Sane* had caused confusion, outrage and unleashed a cultural revolution:

"When I first saw him it was a shock, and yet it was very familiar. It was very necessary. It was something that was needed. It was essential. And like all rock and roll, it was tasteless, it was glamorous, it was perverse, it was fun, it was crass, it was sexy, it was confusing."

Madonna presented the award and Marianne Faithfull sang 'Rebel Rebel' in his honour. But the star himself was absent from the proceedings, maintaining that air of frosty remoteness and teasing mystery that often emanated from an otherwise down to earth, friendly London boy.

Bowie had fought long and hard for recognition. When success came he was still restless, impatient to move on. He'd take unpredictable steps professionally and artistically, all the while undergoing a kaleidoscopic change of styles and images. His appeal remained constant, even as the artist himself sometimes teetered between inspiration and misjudgement. Byrne neatly pictured Bowie as an artist who daringly explored "sexual politics" and successfully combined the disciplines of literature and theatre within the heady freedoms of rock 'n' roll.

This exotic mixture of images, ideas and music ensured "Brand Bowie" would remain both controversial and attractive for five decades and bestow upon him many tributes and accolades. One of the most significant was the choice of music performed at the closing ceremony for the London Olympic Games in August 2012. A huge image of David appeared on the stadium's gigantic projection screen and as part of a tribute to Britain's contribution to pop, a medley of nine Bowie compositions boomed from the PA around the arena and into TV sets around the world.

Millions heard songs that had long since implanted themselves into the collective memories of fans including 'Space Oddity', 'Changes', 'Ziggy Stardust', 'The Jean Genie', 'Rebel, Rebel', 'Diamond Dogs', 'Young Americans', 'Let's Dance' and 'Fashion'. Bowie's 1977 hit '"Heroes"' was also played each time a Team GB member won a medal during the Games.

Once again Bowie himself was absent and did not perform. But his excuse this time it wasn't so much pressing engagements or even his celebrated sense of detachment from the mainstream. He clearly needed to conserve energy. Health issues had already taken their toll on the once wild-eyed boy who was at that time a 65-year-old veteran.

David stopped recording and touring after heart surgery in 2004 and took a full year off after receiving a Grammy 'Lifetime Achievement' Award in February, 2006. But accolades continued to mount up for the artist who had once been Major Tom, Ziggy Stardust, the Cracked Actor and The Thin White Duke. In September 2012 it was announced that a special exhibition was to be staged at London's Victoria & Albert Museum charting his career.

The 'David Bowie Is' exhibition opened in March 2013, and was a huge success, selling out amid a media and public frenzy. The museum's curators announced they had been given access to the Bowie Archive to create his first international exhibition, featuring handwritten lyrics, original costumes and set designs. David was hailed as a Cultural Icon, even though some critics had reservations about a pop singer being showcased at a hallowed temple of the arts and crafts. Such criticism would probably have pleased and amused Bowie, confirming that he was still an outsider and a misunderstood rebel, just like the characters one of his favourite

Previous spread: David Bowie in a photo shoot for *Entertainment Weekly* magazine in Los Angeles, California, June 2002.

Right: Young, handsome and impeccably dressed, David Bowie faces his future as a cultural icon in 1967.

actors, James Dean, portrayed in the movies of his youth. He even
began to distance himself from the project, implying it wasn't
really his concern.

Since his teenage years Bowie had engaged in a search for an
identity and a way of engaging audiences, whether on a stage
or screen, with a personality they could react with or against.
He'd be simultaneously a hero and villain, somebody they'd
love or hate in equal measure. And yet he also appeared as the
eternal lost youth seeking solace and companionship with like-
minded souls before needing to move on, change friends and
alter course.

David Bowie started out leading his own R&B groups in the early
Sixties. Blessed with distinctive good looks, a cool taste in clothes
and penchant for blues singing, he seemed assured of pop idol status.
Record companies somewhat grudgingly took him on, but chart
success eluded him for several frustrating years. It wasn't until 'Space
Oddity' in 1969 that he secured a palpable hit and even then it was
difficult to secure a follow-up and his album sales languished.

As Bowie introduced changes into his life, music and artistic
direction, so his judgements seemed vindicated. He became an
enormous international success at the start of the new decade.
Indeed he came to personify the Seventies, the era of Glam Rock and
the world danced to his tunes 'Starman', 'The Jean Genie', 'Life On
Mars' and 'Rebel Rebel'.

While launching spectacular touring stage shows he
simultaneously unleashed more hit singles 'Rock And Roll Suicide',
'Diamond Dogs', 'Young Americans', 'Fame' and '"Heroes"'. The
early albums were followed by a plethora of exploratory works from
Pin Ups, *Diamond Dogs* and *David Live* towards *Young Americans*,
Station To Station, *Low*, *Heroes*, *Tin Machine* and *Black Tie White Noise*.
Each marked a new epoch in Bowie's progress as he teleported
himself from science fiction imagery towards a more sharply defined
affinity with soul, dance music and even heavy metal.

As a star on a par with rock's other superstars, came the hit
collaborations with John Lennon, Mick Jagger and Freddie Mercury
as 'Fame', 'Dancing In The Street' and 'Under Pressure' hit the
charts. Bowie was also now established as a movie actor in such films
as *The Man Who Fell To Earth* and impressed critics with his stage
performance in *The Elephant Man*.

Years of frantic activity came to an abrupt halt after the release
of *Reality* (2003), although it spiked nearer the end of his life, with

the surprise release of *The Next Day* in 2013 and *Blackstar* in 2016,
released to public and critical acclaim just days before his death.
Bowie had sold some 140 million albums around the world.

Quite an achievement for the androgynous boy from Beckenham
with different coloured eyes, who arrived at the pop ball wearing
nail varnish, bright red hair and a sexy woman's dress. He was the
first pop star to come out and proclaim "I'm gay". Even that was
really just a provocative part of Bowie Plan B.

His ever changing and ideas took him on a long and extraordinary
journey that is beautifully illustrated by this remarkable
compendium of carefully selected photographic images that
seductively chronicle the life of a legend. And now it's time to meet
the real and maybe even the unreal David Bowie – in pictures.

Chris Welch, London 2016.

Left: A cool drink and cool taste in
clothes in this portrait by prominent
photographer Barrie Wentzell, who
shot this in 1973.

Above: The pale-faced David Bowie
studies one of his many heroes (from
many different disciplines), the silent-
era movie actor Buster Keaton.

THE EARLY YEARS

When David Bowie first created waves as his alter ego Ziggy Stardust, the roots and origins of this startling apparition were shrouded in mystery. At least that's how it seemed to his newly acquired fans. So little was known about his 'early years' it all contributed neatly to his mythological status. Perhaps he really was an alien, recently landed on earth in a tin can, whose pre-history didn't exist.

Early in 2012 film researchers scoured the streets of Beckenham, Bromley and West Wickham, in search of locations and to trace memories of the star who had grown up in the South London suburban idyll. Where had he gone to school and where did he play his first gigs? It would all provide useful information for a proposed documentary on the rise of one of the world's most fascinating and revered superstars.

The truth was the singer had been one of an army of young British teenagers thunderstruck by the impact of rock 'n' roll and rhythm and blues. During his formative years he too had desperately sought to the join the ranks of those busy forming their own groups and seeking fame in the pop charts. He was no alien. As far as his earliest loyal supporters were concerned he was "one of us" and clearly possessed of a unique talent and personality. He just had to convince the rest of the world beyond the suburbs.

The boy who would be Bowie was born David Robert Jones at Stansfield Road, Brixton, London on January 8, 1947. His parents were Haywood Stenton 'John' Jones and Margaret 'Peggy' Burns, who had a son Terry, from a previous relationship, who was born in 1937. The couple married in September 1947 and David later went to Stockwell Junior School. In the 1950s the family including half-brother Terry moved to Bromley, Kent and eventually moved into a terraced house in Plaistow Grove in 1955. It was Terry who first encouraged his young half-brother's interest in jazz, poetry and beatnik culture. David was sent to Burnt Ash Junior School then In 1958 he went to Bromley Technical High School where he befriended fellow pupil Peter Frampton, whose father taught at the school. Peter would become lead guitarist with local band The Herd and later achieved fame with Humble Pie and as a solo artist. Another great school friend George Underwood also shared his growing interest in R&B the more authentic strand of American music that that underpinned the roots of rock 'n' roll. "Elvis and Bill Haley are great, but have you heard Chuck Berry and Bo Diddley?" was the cry among hip London teenagers.

George and David had a fight, best described as a skirmish, allegedly over a girlfriend, that resulted in an injury to David's left eye that paralysed the pupil. This caused an odd effect where the normally blue eye appeared brown or green. Despite the knuckle blow from Underwood, the pair remained friends and went on to form their first group together The Konrads, in July 1962.

David Jones sang and played saxophone and the group tried unsuccessfully to get a contract with Decca records. He eventually quit the otherwise promising group in a dispute over musical policy. It seems they didn't share his enthusiasm for playing R&B and preferred to cover Cliff Richard and the Shadows hits instead.

David left school in 1963 and took a job in an advertising agency. Home from work he began playing sax and singing with another Bromley based group The King Bees billed as 'Davie' or 'Davy' Jones. He showed his faith in the group by writing to John Bloom, the washing machine millionaire (who also had a penchant for playing drums), seeking his support. Bloom was impressed by the boy's nerve and recommended him to music biz manager Les Conn.

Previous spread: David Bowie as a true London Boy in the late 1960s.
Left: The young David (seated left), part of the Burnt Ash Junior School football team in 1958.

Right: Sax-toting David with The Konrads in 1963 (left to right) David Crook (drums), Alan Dodds (guitar), Neville Wills (guitar) and George Underwood (vocals).

Les worked hard and secured Davie Jones and The King Bees a contract with Vocalion, a Decca subsidiary, and on June 5, 1964 they released Jones' first single 'Liza Jane' backed by 'Louie Louie Go Home'. The 'A' side reveals Davie singing with exuberant enthusiasm in a remarkably effective post-Elvis blues style about a little girl who causes him much romantic excitement despite being only five foot three. The B-side is less effective and the group tend to plod behind the vocalist. It all sounds like an early Beatles demo reject, only not even that good. Then in September the King Bees released 'You're Holding Me Down' coupled with 'I've Gotta' on the Coral label. When it failed to chart, Davie hooked up with a more promising R&B group from Maidstone called The Manish Boys. They were signed to Parlophone amidst the eager hunt for beat groups during the first wave of Beatlemania and the onslaught of the Rolling Stones. It was an exciting development for 'Davie' and the Manish Boys even went on tour with Gene Pitney, The Kinks and Marianne Faithfull.

Their first single 'I Pity The Fool'/'Take My Tip' (Parlophone) was produced by American Shel Talmy, famed for his work with The Who. The 'A' side was David Jones' first original composition to appear on record. Talmy procured the services of session guitarist Jimmy Page to strengthen the sound with some excellent playing.

David sings in much more relaxed show blues fashion revealing many of his soon to be familiar vocal traits and showing a technique much improved since 'Liza Jane'. The 18-year-old shows himself to be remarkably adept at pitching and phrasing and the jazzy arrangement of 'Take My Tip' is surprisingly sophisticated. Languishing as a B-side it was sadly passed over by the jazz critics of the day, who might have discovered a new talent in their midst and possibly even encouraged the future Bowie to take an entirely different course in his career. This intriguing 'disc' was released on March 5, 1965 but once again a Jones fronted group failed to reach the charts. As a result the Manish Boys promptly split up.

Undaunted, Davy Jones went back into battle with a new single, also produced by Shel Talmy, called 'You've Got A Habit Of Leaving'/'Baby Loves That Way', backed by a fresh group called The Lower Third. It was released by Parlophone on August 20, 1965. The 'A' side reveals a strong Who influence with its clanging Townshend style guitar chords, rumbling drums and Daltrey-esque harmonica. The group even supported The Who on tour.

David's vocals are rather plaintive and appear to be moving towards his melodic Mod phase. 'Baby Loves That Way' has a lilting beat and requires the lead vocalist to battle it out with intrusive backing vocals, while coping with a barrage of 'wordy' lyrics.

Nevertheless such tracks provide a charming footnote and further insight into a clearly brilliant young man's artistic development. It may be 'clear' to us now, but back in the Sixties, London was a fiercely competitive scene. However good looking and talented, how was Jones going to establish himself in the midst of so many already successful groups and artists? He had to do something different, needed direction and above all, a sympathetic, well-connected and encouraging manager. He found Ken Pitt.

Pitt managed many of the top groups of the day who played regularly at London's Marquee Club, such as Manfred Mann and the Mark Leeman Five. At the time David was being managed by Roger Horton, who had previously been a road manager for the Moody Blues. Ken signed David for management and signed him to the Pye label. At the same time, in January 1966, ' Davie Jones' changed his name to David Bowie. It was a romantic, impressive sounding surname, properly pronounced "Bo-wee" and not "Bowy". It was inspired by Jim Bowie, the 19th century American pioneer who had introduced the Bowie knife. The newly adopted name would also help avoid confusion with Davy Jones of The Monkees, the US TV pop group then about to create a worldwide sensation.

It was Ken who advised his protégé to devise a new stage name and the story goes that when visiting Pitt's London apartment one evening the artist told his manager: "By the way, I'm David Bowie now" to which Ken replied casually to this momentous news "That's nice."

At last it seemed Bowie had a good chance of attaining chart placing and music press recognition, all important in the days when weekly papers such as *Melody Maker*, *NME*, *Disc* and *Record Mirror* were the main source of pop news, trends and information. Bowie's first release under his name was 'Can't Help Thinking About Me'/ 'And I Say To Myself' (Pye) and once again he was backed by The Lower Third. The A-side has since been hailed as one of the finest of his early recordings and even achieved a placing in the MM's Top 40. Produced by Tony Hatch it was released in January 1966.

More Bowie singles appeared notably 'Do Anything You Say'/'Good Morning Girl' (Pye), and 'I Dig Everything'/'I'm Not Losing Sleep' (Pye). Sadly these were all flops, the Pye contract was terminated and David ended his association with The Lower Third. He then worked briefly with an outfit called The Buzz that

Left, above: Showboating at Soho's Marquee Club in 1966 with The Buzz. (Left to right) John Hutchinson (guitar), John Eager (drums), Derek Fearnley (bass) and Derrick Boyes (keyboards).

Left: A very young looking David Bowie in a portrait from 1966. He was to play with various combinations of musicians before finding the right mix.

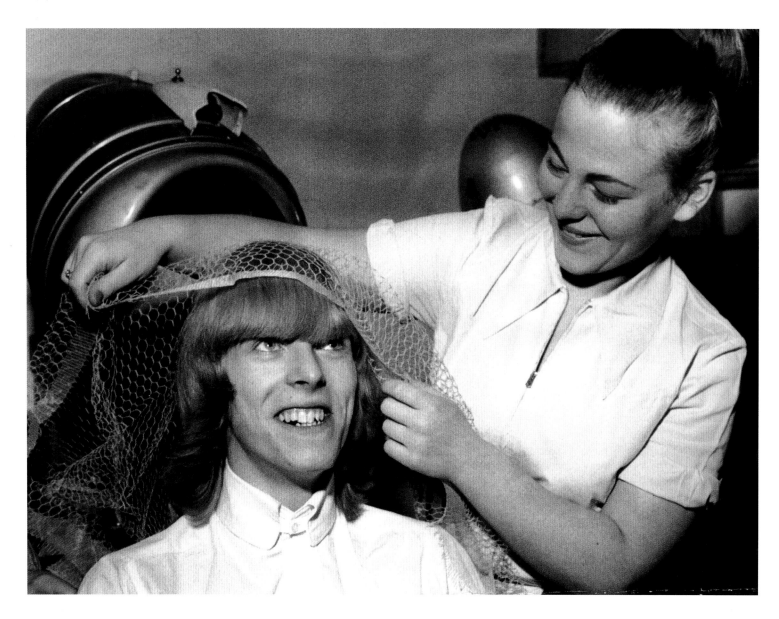

played at the Marquee Club before breaking up in July that year. Bowie would henceforth work as a solo artist, now influenced more by Bob Dylan than Elvis or The Who. He also took film parts, worked as a model and appeared in an experimental movie called *The Image*. While David was improving his social life, going out with dancer Hermione Farthingale, Ken Pitt flew to New York in November 1966, where he met Andy Warhol and Lou Reed, hoping to represent them as their London agent. He brought back to London an album by Lou Reed and the Velvet Underground and played it to Bowie.

By now David was moving on from his R&B group front man stage to becoming a singer/songwriter. His lyrics now reflected his fascination for youthful Mod culture that was an important part of the Soho scene. Pitt now switched David from Pye to Decca, at a time when Decca had passed on many ultimately successful acts including of course The Beatles and closer at home, Manfred Mann. Realising the urgent need to adapt to the

changing UK record business, Decca set up a more progressive label called Deram under the aegis of producer Denny Cordell. It was one of the first so-called 'Indie' labels and helped launch singer/songwriter Cat Stevens, who had hit the charts with 'Matthew And Son'.

Recalls Ken Pitt: "Deram was the brain child of Denny Cordell who was already making some excellent records. I arranged to meet Denny and listened to his ideas. So we signed David on the understanding he would be okay for new modern artists who were doing something different. That worked out very well. Denny Cordell knew this fellow who had come over from

---

Above: David at the BBC in 1965. Hairdresser Sylvia Halliday tends to the singer of The Manish Boys before their appearance on *Gadzooks*.

Right: Once again impeccably dressed, David Bowie in a less formal pose than he was used to making at the time – circa mid-1960s.

America called Tony Visconti and that's how he became a producer for David. Gus Dudgeon also moved over."

At the publishing company Essex Music Tony and engineer Gus were the staff producers. They would make new recordings on behalf of Deram. It was Deram that released David's first solo album called simply *David Bowie* on June 1, 1967. The only claim to fame of the album at the time was it represented the only time a solo artist had been allowed to release a complete album without having previously had a hit record. In fact, attempts were made to get a hit with the single 'Rubber Band'/'London Boys' that came out in December 1966. The A-side was even released in America coupled with 'There Is A Happy Land' – also taken from the LP. Intriguingly good songs with especially fine vocal performances by the 19-year-old, they deserved to be hits but the experimental orchestral backing didn't quite work and the whole package failed to connect with pop hungry teenagers, DJs and mainstream critics, although other musicians and composers recognized the nascent talent at work. On 'Rubber Band' the amusingly wry and witty lyrics are delivered by Bowie with a theatrical flair.

His next single was 'The Laughing Gnome' released on April 14, 1967 and produced by Mike Vernon. It's a droll and comical piece of work that became a favourite among fans of early Bowie but was despised by the Ziggy/Aladdin Sane generation. Bowie's tale of the gnome he tries to send by train to the seaside, only to find he has returned chuckling loudly at the end of Bowie's bed in the morning is enlivened by speeded up tape recording, lots of 'gnome' puns and the voice of the laughing gnome himself provided by the late Gus Dudgeon.

Ironically the track was finally a hit when it was released in September 1973, reaching Number 4 in the UK charts. When Bowie later fronted heavy metal group Tin Machine, members of the audience would delight in yelling requests for 'The Laughing Gnome'.

More important were the album tracks that included such songs as 'Uncle Arthur', 'Sell Me A Coat' and 'Love You Till Tuesday'. The latter was an exceptionally good song and Bowie was now developing a vocal style that incorporated London accents that many felt were influenced by movie star and former pop singer Anthony Newley. In fact Newley felt the same way when he heard the album and he was not pleased. (Newly died in April 19, 1999). Said David later: "I did a lot of Newley things on the first album I

made. I WAS Anthony Newley for a year. He was one of the most talented men England had produced."

'Love You Till Tuesday' received rave reviews in the *Melody Maker* and Ken Pitt planned a video to promote the single that cost him £7000 to make. But despite all their efforts Decca turned down Bowie's next three singles and and finally dropped him from the Deram label.

It was a painful experience for Ken Pitt: "We did some more records that Tony produced and put them up to the regular Monday morning committee meeting at Decca and they turned down three in a row. This even embarrassed one member of the committee. So we left Decca although we had nowhere else to go.

"Decca had a wonderful catalogue of records made in the Fifties and they had a fine classical musical catalogue. They thought it was going to go on like that for ever. You could understand their attitude. I was only allowed to attend the meetings and it was very early in the morning. Two of the committee I never saw because they were hidden behind open newspapers. It was dreadful. So we got out. I felt sorry for the head of the LP department."

Yet earlier Decca had been impressed by the *David Bowie* album. "When the Decca head first heard our album he had said: 'Oh this is the best thing to come into the office since Anthony Newley', which was not what I wanted to hear! I don't believe there was anything on David's records that was influenced by Newley not in the sense that he was doing a deliberate impression. Of course he'd seen Tony's television stuff and liked him very much. Because they were both signed to Essex Music the publishers gave Tony Newley quite a lot of David Bowie's songs and he turned them all down flat! Ha, ha!"

It wasn't the end of the world. In fact it proved a blessing because Bowie was able to move on explore ideas and develop his work with a new label, Mercury. He had already been working on a new song that people began humming as soon as they heard it. It was about an astronaut called Major Tom, who was doomed to be marooned in space. Bowie had just seen the Stanley Kubrick epic *2001: A Space Odyssey* that had made a deep impression on the sci-fi loving movie fan. Real life space travel was also constantly in the news. The end result would be a huge hit single that finally introduced *le vrai* David Bowie to the world as a vibrant, vital and creative 'new' artist. 'Space Oddity' was the song that supplanted the memory of the struggling Sixties R&B groups and even the London Boy of his debut album. Here was a strangely remote yet romantic voice from outer space who encapsulated the mood of the times just as the first American astronauts were about to land on the Moon. David Bowie, the star man was about the land on Planet Earth.

Left: 'Sell Me A Coat'? Wistfully awaiting all the help he can get with 1967 debut album *David Bowie*.

MAJOR TOM

David Bowie seemed adrift in pop space until Major Tom came floating into his life. The late Sixties proved a frustrating period for him in some respects. Yet that didn't stop the artist experimenting, seeking new ideas and gaining valuable experience.

There were also some causes for celebration. His first album had introduced him to the world, won new fans and supporters. His most popular single release 'Love You Till Tuesday' had received a significant music press review in in July 1967. *Melody Maker* proclaimed: "David Bowie is one of the few really original solo singers operating in the theatre of British pop."

The praise continued: "He writes very unusual material, he's good looking and while his voice has Anthony Newly connotations it matters little while he makes fine records of this ilk."

Fine words indeed. Just a shame it wasn't a hit. But now there were more strings to Bowie's bow. If the UK pop market wasn't ready for him, he would take a keener interest in the arts, notably ballet and theatre. He met and studied with Lindsay Kemp, a distinguished mime artist and performed with Kemp in a show called *Pierrot In Turquoise* at a theatre in Oxford in December, 1967.

He still loved the classical music and modern jazz he had discovered as a teenager. At the same time he began paying closer attention to underground American rock. A science fiction fan, Bowie was fascinated by UFOs and also began to take an interest in Buddhism. It was this broad range of interests and eclectic taste that helped make so many British pop artists of the period fascinatingly different and intellectually stimulating.

Recall his manager Ken Pitt: "David was always receptive to new ideas. When we shared a flat in Manchester Street in London, I had a library of books he loved to read and he listened to classical music. Holst's *The Planets* suite became a great favourite. There are many shades and colours in that which you can hear in David's music. But Buddhism was never the result of my influence. I don't think he was really that interested. It became part of his future publicity to say that he was. When he went to RCA after my time as his manager, they said that he went up to Scotland and studied with Buddhists. I do remember him meeting a Buddhist monk at my Curzon Street office. To say that David was gobsmacked is an understatement.

"David himself was going through a slovenly, almost dirty phase. That was because he'd read that one of the tenets of Buddhism was that you shouldn't concern yourself with false exterior images. Then this amazing creature walked in who was wearing a lovely yellow gown, a shaven head and beautiful leather sandals with a jewel between his toes. He was also drenched in glorious perfume. It was very funny."

Ken preferred David as a Mod rather than a Buddhist or even Glam rocker. "As a Mod he was into Vespas and wearing military jackets. He summed up Mod culture with some of his early songs, but that was only because he was observant. He wanted to sing about the Mods he saw hanging around Wardour Street. All these images got lodged in his mind and would come out in songs like 'The London Boys'."

Having dabbled with more than enough R&B groups Bowie now formed a mime troupe called Feathers with girlfriend Hermione Farthingale and his friend John Hutchinson. But it was a short lived affair, as was the relationship with Hermione.

Meanwhile Ken Pitt was assiduously working as Bowie's manager and David had a spare room at his flat that was always available. Although they got on well and had many shared interests, David wasn't always easy to manage. He sometimes disappeared or seemed less interested in continuing the battle for the stardom his manager was trying to gain on his behalf. And there were always other people trying to influence, steer or even surreptitiously take over Bowie's business affairs.

When David met 19-year-old Angela Barnett, she would subsequently have a great impact on his life and career. A vivacious girl and strong willed personality, she was born in Cyprus and educated in America and Switzerland. On arrival in England she began studying at Kingston Polytechnic. David and Angela met at London's Speakeasy club at a press reception for King Crimson, where they were introduced by a mutual acquaintance, Calvin Mark Lee who worked at Mercury Records. Bowie's social circle now included Angela, the talented young American producer Tony Visconti, fellow singer/songwriter Marc Bolan and Marc's girlfriend June Child.

Visconti had begun working on the sessions for the next Bowie album scheduled for release by Mercury. All was looking good until Tony heard the song David had lined up for single release. He took an instant dislike to 'Space Oddity' and declined to work

Previous page: Bowie the curly-haired minstrel in south London's Beckenham Arts Lab days.

Right: "I's got my eyes on you…" David Bowie at Trident Studios in St Martin's Lane in central London, 1970.

on the track. It seemed a wayward decision, but he had his own reasons. He wrote later: "I thought it was a cheap shot to capitalize on the first moon landing." He also felt the style and concept was at odds with the rest of the folk-rock material destined for the album. At first it seemed he might be vindicated as it took a while for the song to achieve its potential.

David had written 'Space Oddity' while making a movie promo for 'Love You Till Tuesday'. Ken Pitt had filmed the new composition too, with David acting out the character of the song's hero, space pilot Major Tom. Ken showed the film to Philips who were greatly impressed, as had been the film crew who Pitt heard humming the melody on the set.

Pitt: "When we came to do 'Space Oddity' we had moved over to Phonogram and Tony Visconti had become the producer. But Tony wasn't very fond of 'Space Oddity'. We respected his business decision. He thought it would be a one-off novelty song, which couldn't be followed up. What he didn't realize was this one-off novelty song would become a huge hit. It all came about because I decided to do a demonstration film showing all that David could do, just as we did with the first Deram album. I wanted something that would show him visually and he could do whatever he wanted on this film. I could then take it round to the BBC and say 'Would you please watch this'."

Ken asked David and director Malcolm Thompson to come up with a new piece of material to add to the film. Malcolm later phoned Pitt to say: 'I think he's got it. David has just played me something which is just what you're looking for.'

The pair returned to the Manchester Street flat to unveil the piece. Ken: "David sat on the edge of my chaise longue and sang me 'Space Oddity'. It was incredible. The first recording was a demo disc and the next recording was the backing track for the film. It was quite a fight to get it accepted. It really had nothing to do with the space mission Apollo 11. I was just concerned with getting a song for the film.

"We didn't know much about the NASA mission although David was always interested in space. That summer the Rolling Stones gave a free concert in London's Hyde Park and the DJ played 'Space Oddity'. It was being broadcast to thousands of people in the park. It was also played on TV. I heard people singing it in the streets and Major Tom became a popular character."

The finished recording begins with solemn acoustic guitars chords and the sombre, immortal opening line "Ground control

Left: "Ground control to Major Tom…"
Bowie in concert in 1970 at the
Roundhouse in north London.

to Major Tom". Instructions to the pilot follow, as he is about to be launched into space. Once above the earth, the orbiting with Major Tom gets out of his capsule for a daring spacewalk. He reports back.

Tom's description of his space suit as a "tin can" is a Bowie-esque touch of humour that actually underscores the gravity of the situation; or rather the lack of gravity, as Major Tom is marooned in space due to faulty circuits. Doomed to float far above the moon, he sends his final messages back to Ground Control professing love to his wife and a final report that "Planet Earth is blue and there's nothing I can do".

The arrangement is brilliantly conceived and the production is like a movie soundtrack with its use of unusual instruments. Mysterious, slightly out of tune chords are provided by session man Rick Wakeman using a Mellotron while Bowie adds spacey effects with the newly invented Stylophone organ.

'Space Oddity' was profoundly clever and despite Ken Pitt's reservations about Bowie's alleged influences, it was clearly topical as America's real life astronauts were scheduled to land on the moon that year. Indeed, on July 20, 1969 Neil Armstrong took his famous first small step for man and giant leap for Mankind. Despite his producer's reservations, the record was ultimately a hit and a giant leap for David Bowie.

In Visconti's absence the track was produced by the late Gus Dudgeon, an engineer who got to know David while working with producer Mike Vernon at Deram. Gus had a good sense of humour and had supplied the high pitched voice of the notorious 'Laughing Gnome'. When he first heard the demo recording of 'Space Oddity' he thought it was "incredible" and gladly accepted the job of producing the single while Tony concentrated on the rest of the album.

As well as Rick Wakeman on keyboards, the backing musicians were Mick Wayne (guitar), Herbie Flowers (bass) and Terry Cox (drums). Dudgeon recalled later that Wakeman arrived late for the session, having travelled to the studio via the London Underground. But he quickly got down his part in two takes while David played the Stylophone using a stylus to pick out notes on the tiny keyboard.

A string arrangement was provided by Paul Buckmaster and the whole shebang was released in stereo. When the record was played at the Rolling Stones' legendary free concert in Hyde Park on July 5, 1969 – designated as a tribute to Brian Jones who had died a few days earlier – it seemed perfectly in tune with the strangely eerie mood of the day.

The summer of 1969 was full of historic moments both on earth and in outer space. Yet 'Space Oddity' only got to Number 48 in the UK in September and completely failed to dent the US chart.

It reached the point where the record company withdrew the single after it had spent just one week in the chart.

Help was at hand and radio DJs began to play it consistently arousing interest way beyond Hyde Park and the London hippie scene. 'Space Oddity' was hastily reissued. At last the public woke up and the record launched itself into a trajectory that took it to Number 5 in the UK at the end of the month. It stayed in the singles charts for a further 13 weeks.

Ken Pitt: "Although 'Space Oddity' began to climb up the charts and got to Number 5, I was told it was deliberately squashed in America because of the sadness of a space man disappearing in a 'tin can' just when they were sending one of their own men to the moon. I guess they thought 'Space Oddity' was wryly ironic. And of course it was."

The success should have set a seal on the Bowie-Pitt partnership but events would prove otherwise.

Ken: "We had a very good relationship that worked well until outside people and predators appeared on the scene and began to

interfere. It happens so often. It was a shame. People were saying 'I can do better for you.'

"Despite the later arrival of Ziggy Stardust most people still think of 'Space Oddity' when they think of David Bowie. It appealed to all age groups and tastes and Ziggy Stardust only appealed to rock 'n' rollers. A lot of David's younger fans think he started with Ziggy Stardust. Talent and notoriety are quite different. They might remember this tricky fellow with red hair but they wouldn't remember what he did. Everyone still remembers David Bowie as the boy who hit with 'Space Oddity'."

In its wake came pop stardom for Bowie, the man who had been signed to no less than five different labels and had been on the fringes of the music biz for some six years. David was in demand for TV, radio and live appearances and the music press now clamoured for interviews.

The song would have an extraordinarily long life. When 'Space Oddity' was rereleased by RCA in October, 1975 it became David's first UK Number One hit. It also got to Number 15 in the *Billboard* chart in February 1973, his first American chart entry, despite a slew of earlier British hits.

Gus Dudgeon, who had the honour of producing such a ground-breaking single, went on to produce two other 'space' hits including 'I'm The Urban Spaceman' (1968), for the Bonzo Dog Doo Dah Band and 'Rocket Man'(1972) by Elton John. Sadly, after a distinguished career, Gus and his wife Sheila died in a car crash on July 21, 2002.

During that exciting summer of 1969 David and Angela became an item and lived together at David's mum's home, an apartment at Haddon Hall, a Victorian Gothic mansion in Southend Lane, Beckenham, Kent, now demolished. Bowie had also stayed as a lodger at flat with girlfriend Mary Finnegan and, together with a group of friends, they set up a Folk Club at the Three Tuns public house on Beckenham High Street. Sessions took place each Sunday night where David sang and read poetry and invited guest artists. The club was called Growth and attracted large audiences.

In May the club was renamed the Arts Lab with the aim of encouraging more young people to expand their minds and creativity. He even organized a free festival in a Beckenham park that took place on August 16, just a few days after the death of his father on August 5. Bowie enthused to *Melody Maker* about the Arts Lab movement and described his own as: "The best in the country. There isn't one pseud involved. All the people are real,

---

Left: One size fits all. David's space suit for the man about town. Photographed at the studio of artist Dante Leonard in London in 1969.

Right: Bowie makes a soft landing after his trip to outer space.
Overleaf: Bowie in Hamburg, Germany for a television appearance in 1968.

like labourers or bank clerks. It started out as a folk club and arts labs generally have a bad reputation as pseud places.

"There's a lot of talent in the green belt and a load of tripe in Drury Lane. I think the arts lab movement is extremely important and should take over from the youth club as a social service. The people who come are completely pacifist and we get a lot of co-operation from the police. They are more than helpful. Respect breeds respect. We've got a few greasers who come and a few skinheads who are just as enthusiastic. Poets and artists come along and we have our own light show. And I never knew there were so many sitar players in Beckenham."

David sang regularly at the Three Tuns where girls gazed at him with ill-concealed adoration. Local lads too were inspired to take up the guitar. More than 40 years later many a suburban husband retained fond memories of the star who once sang in their midst alongside such guests as Peter Frampton, Dave Cousins, Steve Harley, Tony Visconti, Rick Wakeman and Mick Ronson. Even Lionel Bart, the famed composer of the musical *Oliver!*, who had first tipped off Ken Pitt about the existence of Davy Jones in the early Sixties, made a special appearance.

Bowie's own appearances at the Arts Lab were commemorated with the unveiling of a plaque at the Three Tuns, that had become the Rat & Parrot by the time a special ceremony was organized by local residents and held on December 6, 2001.

Ken Pitt was now observing David's life on the cultural fringes from afar. Even before the success with 'Space Oddity' he'd become worried by his behaviour. "He started going missing. His irate mum would be on the phone. 'Have you seen David? Are you expecting him?' He disappeared for two or three days and his parents were worried. It turned out that he'd been staying with one of Lindsay Kemp's dancers who was a very lovely girl. Then he moved in with Hermione Farthingale. I rather hoped that relationship would develop because she was an extremely nice girl and very level headed. He went to live with her in Kensington with three or four other people. We started doing the film *Love You Till Tuesday* while he was there."

However she considered David's life style was too erratic, so he came back to Manchester Street and stayed at Ken's flat once more or found solace and company back in Beckenham.

Ken: "I didn't go to the Free Festival in the Beckenham park. By then Angela had come on the scene and then we were really in trouble, all round. Everything was a mystery about Angela. She was an American whose parents were living in Cyprus where her father was an engineer. She had been to a girl's school in Switzerland. She had come to London and was working in a travel agency in Queensway. The mystery was how did she get to know David? She knew a fellow who ran Mercury Records in London and had an office opposite hers. She had been going out with this fellow and then suddenly someone else came on her scene."

The Arts Lab was fun but suddenly it was back to serious business. At the end of the year Bowie was invited to take part in a tour with Humble Pie, the new 'supergroup' that included Steve Marriott and his old pal Peter Frampton. David played a solo acoustic set and it was reported that skinhead rock fans booed his performance, even when he played 'Space Oddity'. Not much mind expansion there.

It might have been the hostility of some audiences that encouraged David to consider burying his own vulnerable personality inside a specially created uber image. If he was going to be a star on stage, he might as well be a truly outrageous figure that would stun the world.

At the same time he had to endure the spectacle of his friend Marc Bolan cheekily moving on up from his acoustic adventures with the quirky Tyrannosaurus Rex, towards becoming a fully-fledged rock star. All hope was now pinned on the second album *David Bowie* (Philips) released on November 4, 1969. It would include such intriguing new compositions as 'Unwashed And Somewhat Slightly Dazed', 'God Knows I'm Good' and 'Memories Of A Free Festival'. It seemed as if Bowie was finally emerging to express his freedom and independence.

The second Bowie album underwent a few changes to its release schedule. It was issued under the title *Man Of Words, Man Of Music* (Mercury) in the US in November 1969 then re-released in the UK retitled *Space Oddity* (RCA) in October 1972 and containing a longer version of the 1969 hit single as the opening track.

Next came 'Unwashed And Somewhat Slightly Dazed', a lengthy performance delivered in menacing, angry tones as David yells and whoops above the jamming guitars. A harmonica wails above a Bo Diddley beat and the overall effect is like a rather wild R&B night at the Marquee Club where David used to go and see bands like The Yardbirds and his favourite singer Keith Relf.

The mood is more mellow and the lyrics are more discernible on 'Letter To Hermione' a poetic and touching love song dedicated to former girlfriend Hermione Farthingale, who had left him during the filming of the *Love You Till Tuesday* movie. He says with charming courtesy 'I'm not quite sure what I'm supposed to do, so I'll just write some love to you.'

'Cygnet Committee' is a remarkable piece of work with Bowie digging at great length into his own lyrics with a painful sincerity. He laments "I gave them life…they drained my very soul…" It's a personal testament during which he seems to protest at the way his work in the cause of the hippies and Arts Lab movement wasn't always appreciated. After all it was he who had "Praised their efforts to be free…words of strength and sympathy". The declamation

reaches a bolero climax as David roars "I want to believe ... I want to live!" An excitingly intense performance, but it may well have gone over the heads of many a DJ, A&R man and teenybopper.

However 'Janine' that brightened up the second side of the original LP showed Bowie's extraordinary gift at adapting different styles, while retaining his own distinguishing vocal features. The crucial line "If you took an axe to me, you'd kill another man not me at all" has some of the dark humour and angst of a Johnny Cash song. 'An Occasional Dream' has touches of John Lennon and The Beatles with its use of flutes and recorders adding a quirky melancholy flavour more Merseyside than Thames valley.

'The Wild Eyed Boy From Freecloud' promises more than it delivers although Bowie sings with all the passion of a cabaret artist on a track released as the B-side of the 'Space Oddity' single in July 1969. 'The Wild Eyed Boy' was one of Bowie's own favourite compositions from the album and it certainly worked better when performed live. The lyrics deal with his feelings of being an outsider, always on the edge of events rather than being at the centre, which of course, as it turns out, wasn't true. Bowie was rapidly becoming the centre of the universe for many smitten followers, lovers and disciples.

'God Knows I'm Good' is a more straight forward, Dylan-esque ballad of a tired old lady caught shop lifting inside a supermarket and protesting her innocence and essential honesty.

The final track 'Memory Of A Free Festival' is a requiem for his Arts Lab days and the free festival in his local recreation ground. "It was ragged and naïve... it was heaven" he intones. "I kissed a lot of people that day..." The festive mood is recaptured in a medley of chaotic noises that gradually evolve into a rocking riff built around the mantra "The sun machine is coming down and we're gonna have a party."

The *David Bowie* album is full of intriguing, highly personal insights into the state of Bowie's mind and mood. But it is also a rather sprawling, chaotic collection of songs that only served to further confuse potential audiences. While the outstanding tracks are 'Space Oddity' (for which he received an Ivor Novello Award) and 'Cygnet Committee' at least the rest added to the air of mystery and fuelled fascination with the wild eyed boy from Beckenham.

1969 ended with David appearing at a charity concert at the London Palladium in November on a bill with Dusty Springfield and Tiny Tim. 1970 began with a trip to Scotland to film a TV show with Lindsay Kemp. Recalls Ken Pitt: "David already wanted to be an actor and was capable of doing many different things. He really wanted to write musicals. It was all down to evolution and David was evolving constantly, sometimes from day to day. It was difficult to keep up with his train of thought. He used to store things up like his later idea for Ziggy Stardust."

Bowie's next step was to seal his relationship with Angela Barnett who had briefly returned to Cyprus after an argument with David. He lured her back by proposing marriage. In February he worked with guitarist Mick Ronson on a variety of projects that would include forming the band Hype with Tony Visconti on bass and John Cambridge on drums. They performed their first gig at the BBC's Paris Cinema in London. On February 22 Hype played at the Roundhouse in London's Chalk Farm supporting Country Joe & The Fish.

Hype performed in costume for the first time and the idea was for each band member to adopt a different persona. Bowie was 'Rainbowman', Tony Visconti on bass guitar was 'Hypeman', Mick Ronson was 'Gangersterman' and drummer John Cambridge was 'Cowboyman'. It was a daring idea that didn't go down too well with the audience, but a precedent was set and the future looked Glam. John Cambridge would leave Hype after another fraught gig in Croydon and was replaced by Mick Ronson's friend from Yorkshire, drummer Woody Woodmansey.

Amidst all the musical activity David took the plunge and on March 20 he married Angela Barnett at a registry office in Bromley, in a quiet ceremony attended by his mother. That same month the relationship with manager Ken Pitt seemed to be foundering and David finally announced he wanted to manage himself. In the event he was recommended to approach a lawyer, one Tony Defries who now became Bowie's new manager. Simultaneously work began on the artist's third effort *The Man Who Sold The World* – one that would cause a sensation. Released in April it came to be regarded by fans and critics as the first truly indispensable Bowie album. It was produced by Tony Visconti who also played bass, with Mick Ronson on guitar and Woody Woodmansey on drums.

However, what excited immediate attention was the striking LP cover photograph of the singer. Clad in a beautiful salmon pink and blue satin dress, wearing knee length boots with long hair flowing over his shoulders, he lay stretched out as if posing for a pre-Raphaelite portrait. A deck of cards scattered across the floor, hinted at some kind of game designed to further intrigue any witness to this entrancing scene. Even before a single stylus had hit a groove to play the music, millions of record buyers would want to know – who was this remarkable young man, or was it a girl? The mystique of David Bowie was born and his career would enter a stunning phase.

Opposite left: David with mother, Mrs Margaret Jones and new wife Angie on their wedding day at Bromley Register Office, March 20, 1970.

Right: David in 1967. The original story accompanying this photograph was about how David had received his first fan letter from the USA.

THE RISE AND FALL OF ZIGGY STARDUST

Ziggy Stardust was just a year away when David Bowie entered a period of turbulence, change and creativity. Newly married and all set with a replacement manager, he was plunging towards a rock 'n' roll future. While his own methods and decisions remained spontaneous and impulsive, with Tony Defries taking the business reins, there was now a determined push toward realizing Bowie's potential as a megastar.

David also had a strong team of backing musicians including the lads from Yorkshire, Mick Ronson and Mick 'Woody' Woodmansey, who had been together in their band The Rats. When Woody received a call from David asking him to replace John Cambridge in The Hype he described encountering the Bowie milieu as: "A culture shock. We were Northerners who lived in jeans and patches. Long hair was considered dressing up for us. David wore red shoes with hand painted blue stars. He'd painted them on himself. He was an artist 24/7 and everything he did was to create an effect on stage and he meant it as well."

Although Woody came to appreciate what the singer was trying to achieve, there were moments of stress and disagreement. During the recording of *The Man Who Sold The World* Woody and Mick had an altercation with Bowie and briefly left the band. They headed back to Hull missing out a gig at Leeds University. Woody: "We were in the studio when David started singing like Marc Bolan. We couldn't cope with that and I said I couldn't go on stage with David doing that. So David did the gig on his own."

The pair reformed The Rats but the errant musicians were convinced to come back South along with fellow Rat and bass guitarist Trevor Bolder. Henceforth Bowie's band developed a stronger identity. All three moved into Haddon Hall in Beckenham and found themselves caught up in an exotic new life style.

Sessions for *The Man Who Sold The World* at Trident Studios in London's Soho were completed during April and May 1970 but the album wasn't released until April the following year. It was unveiled with the startling cover portrait of Bowie in his silk dress, bought for him by Angela from Mr. Fish for £300. This artistic statement was accepted with amusement and surprise at home. In America however the record company offices reverberated to cries of dismay. As a result the U.S. release had a black and white photo of a high-kicking Bowie on the cover instead. When asked about his more sensational outfit Bowie replied with a chuckle that it was "A man's dress". It was meant to be decorative and "pure theatre." But he was annoyed at the interference with the artwork and subsequently left Mercury for RCA following intense management negotiations.

In January 1971 he embarked on his first promotional visit to the United States where he embarked on a round of press and TV interviews. In New York he was invited to meet such luminaries as Andy Warhol, Iggy Pop and Lou Reed. David was particularly interested in the sounds being created by Lou Reed and the Velvet Underground that became a considerable influence on his own musical direction.

Whatever the fuss about the 'dress' LP cover, it was of course Bowie's music that mattered. The album's opening track 'The Width Of A Circle' is a powerful eight minute saga, its impact heightened by the intense vocals battling the roar of the group. Ronson's guitar sets the mood with a stirring series of riffs and exploding chords while David is manic as he launches into a psychotic freak out with the proclamation "I ran across a monster who was sleeping by a tree…I looked and frowned because the monster was me."

After a stirring guitar solo the tempo picks up and Bowie sings of a homoerotic sexual encounter during which he intones "He swallowed his pride and puckered his lips, my knees were shaking, my cheeks aflame…do it again, do it again…"

'All The Madmen' that follows was written at Haddon Hall while Bowie was undergoing painful personal experiences including the death of his father, the split with the paternal Ken Pitt and the increased suffering of his mentally ill half-brother Terry then being treated in hospital.

Acoustic guitars launch Bowie into an introspective monologue as he puts himself into the place of a hospital patient undergoing painful procedures. "Day after day they take some brain away" he sings in an unreconstructed South London accent rendered chilling by the disturbing imagery.

'Black Country Rock' is a merry ditty suspiciously like a mockery of T. Rex, the group that had brought success for his pal/rival Marc

---

Previous page: A pouting Bowie launches his most iconic image, as Ziggy Stardust gets his boots on in London, June 1972.

Right: Shoulder power as the Glam Rock era dawned and David Bowie took a step in the direction of looking like someone from another planet.

"The Man" he meets upon the stairs is perceived as his alter ego, a friend from his past who had died long ago. An attractive tune, it was covered by pop singer Lulu in 1973 and again in 1993 by Kurt Cobain with Nirvana on their *MTV Unplugged In New York* album (1994). Bowie himself revived the song in 1979 on the US TV show *Saturday Night Live*.

Closing track 'The Supermen' reflects Bowie's interest in the writings of German philosopher Frederick Wilhelm Nietzsche who came up with the idea of a superman in his work *Also Sprach Zarathustra*. The author propagated the idea that "Nothing is true, everything is allowed" before succumbing to an early death after suffering 12 years of insanity.

David performs his stage demon act with a mad and devilish intensity as he describes the supermen who are "Guardians of a loveless isle gloomy browed with superfear." In many respects this was a dress rehearsal for Ziggy Stardust, all-powerful rock star.

The Man Who Fell To Earth was a disappointingly slow seller. But there was one more pre-Ziggy album to come. *Hunky Dory* released a year later in December 1971 was a big leap forward. By now David was signed to RCA and Tony Defries' company Mainman was assiduously promoting the new star.

Life seemed better and there was more cause for celebration

when David and Angela's son Duncan Zowie Haywood Jones was born in Bromley hospital on May 28. As a grown man Duncan would achieve fame in his own right as the director of hit sci-fi movie *Moon* (2009). Like many of his father's song the story of the film explored a man's impending madness, foreboding and sense of isolation.

Sessions for *Hunky Dory* began in July and was notable for its improved recording quality with production now in the capable hands of Ken Scott. He ensured Bowie's vocals rang forth with a new clarity. This was immediately evident on 'Changes' the brightly funky opening number. Surprisingly this now highly familiar song wasn't a chart hit single despite considerable airplay.

The changes he refers to dwell on the turmoil of his past life as well as the effects of the ongoing Vietnam war on society. Ironically, while this track released as a single in January 1972 failed to chart, the next number 'Oh! You Pretty Things' was a hit for Peter Noone, formerly of Herman's Hermits. His version, kindly donated by David, leapt to Number 12 in the UK. Meanwhile as 'Changes' was struggling to make an impact as a single, David played a rare one-off gig at the Lanchester Arts Festival in Coventry, having ditched the slog of unproductive tours at unsuitable venues. He was backed by Ronson, Bolder and Woodmansey and for once the audience was right on. No more boos, only cheers. Soon he would be experiencing a form of "Bowiemania" that would rival Marc Bolan's "T. Rextasy".

'Oh! You Pretty Things' starts with the cheeky exhortation "Wake up you sleepy head, put on some clothes, shake up your bed". It starts with some heavy piano chords from the composer as he grapples with thoughts of the latent potential of mankind destined to become Homo Superior rather than mere Homo Sapien.

'Eight Line Poem' that follows has a country rock vibe as the guitar and piano duet with slow paced emphasis behind Bowie's curiously contorted vocals.

One of David's best loved and most popular compositions was the striking 'Life On Mars?' It would become a Number 3 in the UK charts in July 1973 and the line "look at those cavemen go" would echo around planet Earth. Strings and tympani bring the piece to a striking conclusion.

'Kooks' is a sweet, touching song about himself and Angela as the eagerly expectant parents of Duncan Jones, about to be born to "a couple of kooks" . They busy themselves buying the baby "lots of things to keep him warm and dry". The song is full of sound advice, such as not picking fights at school with bullies. David later dismissed the song as slushy and sentimental. Yet it harks back to that first *David Bowie* album of 1967, with its quirky simplicity.

'Quicksand' has gentle acoustic guitar accompaniment as David delves into a 'silent film' setting while peppering the lyrics with references to Aleister Crowley the legendary magician and sundry

other notorious figures. The main theme is about loss of personal powers and the eternal contest between light and darkness.

'Fill Your Heart' is a whimsical composition by American singer/songwriter Biff Rose with strings and a saxophone solo courtesy of the Thin White Duke. It's pretty thin stuff with David sounding like he's auditioning for a role in a Punch & Judy Show, although Rick Wakeman provides musical relief at the piano. 'Andy Warhol' is meant a tribute to the great artist although its general air of levity apparently upset the recipient. No doubt the studio banter and laughter generated by a discussion about the pronunciation of his name ("Warhol as in holes" chortled David) became a sore point. It was the sort of fame nobody wanted even for 15 minutes.

'Song For Bob Dylan' also went down badly with the man it intended to praise, perhaps because Bowie neatly recaptured many of Dylan's vocal traits while describing him as having a voice "like sand and glue". Much better is 'Queen Bitch', a return to rock 'n' roll and camp imagery with its tales of gay love and cross dressing. Mick Ronson's guitar brings a joyful exuberance to proceedings as David disparages a rival's hat.

Hunky Dory concludes with 'The Bewlay Brothers', a disturbing look at the relationship with his half-brother that involves introspection and self-analysis in an increasing strange and frightening way. The whole album is awash with such conflicting ideas and ebbs and flows with touches of genius.

But now it was time to concentrate the mind on one unifying concept *The Rise And Fall Of Ziggy Stardust And The Spiders From Mars*.

Bowie's fifth album would become one of his most famous and successful. The underlying concept was to take the idea of fabrication and the way it had come to dominate popular culture. He later claimed that "Realism and honesty had become boring to many jaded people by the early Seventies".

Bowie's idea was to create a persona that was unearthly and unreal and then live it out in real life. It was his way of solving his own identity problems. The album title could be seen as Bowie's riposte to such portentous master works as the Beatles' *Sgt. Pepper's Lonely Hearts Club Band* and Rolling Stones' *Their Satanic Majesties Request*.

It might also be viewed as a running commentary on the rise and rise of Marc Bolan and T. Rex now dominating the charts with 'Hot Love', 'Get It On', 'Jeepster', 'Telegram Sam' and 'Metal Guru'. Marc was the king of Glam Rock, clad in satins, feathers and sparkly make up. Bowie hadn't enjoyed a big hit since 'Space Oddity' in 1969.

Left: Ziggy and the Spiders in the studio posing for portraits in London, November 1972. Left to right: Guitarist Mick Ronson, bassist Trevor Bolder, David Bowie and drummer Mick 'Woody' Woodmansey.

Although Marc Bolan seemed like the obvious role model for 'Ziggy', Bowie later explained that a British rock 'n' roll singer called Vince Taylor had really inspired the concept. Vince was born Brian Maurice Holden in London in 1939 and grew up in America. Returning to London in the Sixties he began singing at the 2Is coffee bar in Soho and formed his own group The Playboys.

He later moved to France where he dressed in black leather and became a rock 'n' roll star rivalling Johnny Hallyday. He enjoyed a hit with 'Brand New Cadillac' and was hailed as the French Elvis Presley. However drink and drugs took their toll and his life and career descended into chaos. He became obsessed with religion, wore white robes, preached the Bible on stage and proclaimed himself the new Messiah. Bowie met Taylor in London and was impressed by his crazed life style and saw him as a cult genius. Vince performed intermittently until moving to Switzerland to work as a maintenance engineer where he found greater happiness far away from rock 'n' roll. He died from cancer in August 1991 aged 52.

Bowie had long been intrigued by the story of the mythical rock 'n' roll idol, sadly all but forgotten in England. David: "Vince Taylor was the inspiration for Ziggy. He was slowly going crazy."

Another important influence was obscure American singer The Legendary Stardust Cowboy, who had a small hit with his bizarre single 'Paralyzed' in 1968. It is now perceived as a classic of the 'psychobilly' genre and became a great favourite with Bowie. Real name Norman Carl Odom, the Texas born 'Cowboy' proclaimed he had wanted to visit Mars since childhood and long dreamt of being famous. He certainly became so after Bowie appropriated 'Stardust' for Ziggy and 'The Ledge' as he was known to fans returned the compliment by recording his own version of 'Space Oddity'.

Ziggy could also be seen as an amalgam of many other real life burnt out idols from Jimi Hendrix to Jim Morrison, not forgetting Andy Warhol who had conceived the idea of the star maker, bringing celebrity, however briefly, to the masses.

The Warhol influence was at work when the cast of *Pork*, a stage show that depicted life at Warhol's New York base The Factory came to London. Cherry Vanilla and Wayne County took part in the show sat the Round House where they sported dyed hair and showers of glitter. At the time Bowie was still

Bolan too had once been a hippie underground idol. Now he was a pop star idolized by teenyboppers. Perhaps Ziggy Stardust could achieve for Bowie the same level of fame and adoration, in a bibbety bobbity way.

There were several strands to the creation of Ziggy involving various people, influences and experiments along the way. Superficially the Ziggy 'look' simply involved David sporting dyed red hair, tight trousers and boots. And of course he had to be 'gay' as he informed *Melody Maker* writer Michael Watts in a memorable interview. "I'm gay and always have been even when I was David Jones." It was the quote that put the seal of success on the master plan. Ziggy/Bowie became the star whose fame spread around the world. However, aware of the effect this might have on his nearest and dearest he took the trouble to phone his mother and reassure her none it was true.

Back in the pop world, he was helped on his way by Suzi Fussey who created the 'Ziggy' hairstyle. She worked in a salon opposite the Three Tuns in Beckenham in Arts Lab days and now became Bowie's wardrobe assistant and the Spiders' hairdresser on Ziggy tours. She also became Mick Ronson's personal assistant and the couple later married. The clothes for Ziggy and the Spiders were devised by influential Japanese designer Kansai Yamamoto during a visit to London and Bowie's keen interest Japan's Kabuki theatre provided further incentives.

wearing hippie outfits on stage during this period, so *York* made quite a sartorial impression.

Among his other achievements, Warhol had encouraged Lou Reed and the Velvet Underground back in New York. So in London Bowie devised a group he called, rather inauspiciously, Arnold Corns. This was intended to back fashion designer Freddi Buretti, billed as vocalist 'Rudi Valentino'. In April 1971 Bowie produced two singles by this outfit for the B&C label with himself singing anonymously on the first one, 'Moonage Dream' and 'Hang On To Yourself' – songs that later appeared on the *Ziggy* album. Valentino sang on the second release 'Hang On To Yourself' coupled with 'Looking For A Friend'.

Both singles failed to chart but it had been a useful experiment, bringing together backing musicians and future Spiders Ronson, Woodmansey and Bolder. These Spiders were of course The Rats who eventually went into action at Trident Studios for the 'Ziggy' sessions under the watchful ears of producer Ken Scott, taking over from Tony Visconti who was now fully absorbed with T.Rex.

There was no set plan to make a concept album as such but Bowie certainly had a plenty of songs ready. At one stage the album was going to be called *Round and Round*, which would have been truly boring. Sessions took place even before *Hunky Dory* was released and continued into January 1972. The completed 'Ziggy' would eventually be issued under its full title on June 6, 1972.

Bowie would later confess that *The Rise And Fall Of Ziggy Stardust...* was a fractured piece of work and the Spiders From Mars weren't really represented sufficiently as a proper band. But the idea took hold of the public's imagination helped by an attractive and mysterious LP cover design.

This shows Bowie in dyed blonde hair and clad in a green jump suit and boots, clutching a guitar and posing amongst a pile of boxes in a Soho alley, with an illuminated sign proclaiming 'K.West' above his head. The rear cover shot has Bowie with hands on hips ensconced inside a red London telephone box. These images were originally shot on a rainy night in black and white by photographer Brian Ward, who later tinted them to add garish colour.

The prominent 'K.West' sign seemed to intimate a 'quest' was underway, but it was just the name of furriers based at 23 Heddon Street, a turning off Regent Street. This location became a place of

pilgrimage for Ziggy devotees just as Abbey Road had become for Beatles fans.

The album sold an impressive 8,000 copies in its first week of release and Ziggy and the Spiders performed two sell-out shows at London's Rainbow Theatre on August 19 and 20, 1972 where they were supported by Roxy Music. It was Glam rock heaven. Bowie made a grand entrance amidst clouds of smoke wearing a silver suit with his hair bright scarlet and introducing himself with cheery "Hello, I'm Ziggy Stardust and these are the Spiders From Mars". At the climax of the show he was joined by Lindsay Kemp dressed as an angel.

Eventually Bowie took off his silver suit and posed on a high platform clad only in red underwear, where he sang 'Starman' under the beams of light from a revolving glitter ball. This entire extravaganza was eagerly watched by an audience that included Alice Cooper, Lou Reed, Elton John and Mick Jagger.

In September that year Bowie set off on an American tour that included a show at New York's Carnegie Hall. He received excellent reviews, although not all the US shows sold out.

The 'Ziggy' album that sparked all the excitement had been

Left: David Bowie in sneering, snarling Ziggy Stardust form, photographed by Mick Rock at the Beverly Hills Hotel, Los Angeles in

Right: David with 12-string guitar at Friars Aylesbury music club on January 29, 1972. It was at this venue (on a different night) that Ziggy

later state that it took just one week to lay down all the tracks. "Most of the songs were done in one or two takes. That way we could go for it and nail them down. We were all pushing in the same direction with the same message. We wanted it to have a live feel and sound good with no embarrassing bits. That freshness somehow got onto vinyl. 'Ziggy' made David a superstar and the whole concept was based on his ideas.

"I remember when Mick and I had to go to Liberty's to get material for the Spiders costumes. We were wandering around wondering what we were doing in the store looking at blue, pink and gold material. Then David did some drawings in the lounge back home and he called us and said 'These are going to be the outfits.'

"It was totally unreal. Mick was supposed to wear gold and me and Trevor were going 'Who is going to be pink?' Well Trevor had dark hair and looked good in blue. Then Angela looked at me and said: 'You have to be a real man to be in pink.'

"Mick then said 'I'm a musician. I've got friends. I'm not going on stage looking like that.' He packed his bags and left. He went to Beckenham station. David said to me: 'Go and get him.' I sat on

the platform with him and explained what it was all about, even though I wasn't fully convinced. It could all have gone horribly wrong. But we took a risk and it took guts by David to persevere with the idea".

Mick and Woody returned to the Ziggy fold and later David took them to a West End theatre and told them to watch the stage lighting. Woody: "Rock bands didn't take big lighting rigs out in those days. If they did have lights it was just red or green and that was the climax. David wanted to use lighting creatively to add atmosphere to help explain what the songs were all about."

Woody remembers the writing routine and domestic arrangements at Haddon Hall: "David's mother brought us tea in bed one Sunday morning. Mick was asleep on the landing when

Above: David Bowie interviewed at his home in Beckenham on April 24, 1972. He is wearing the same outfit as on the cover of *Ziggy Stardust…*

Above right: David Bowie arrives for a concert at the Odeon, Hammersmith, London in 1973. It was to be an eventful night.

David's mum arrived with the tea. He woke up and leaped up completely naked out of his sleeping bag."

Fortified with tea, work continued apace. Woody: "When David wrote the songs he played them to us on acoustic guitar. Then we had to play them as rock songs. First David would play some piano and then he'd sit in the lounge and you'd hear him play guitar. Then he'd shout 'Woody, come and have a listen,' and he'd play us a new song. Every song was good in that period and he was on a roll. Trevor and I had to find a beat that would bring the songs to life.

"And so we became Spiders From Mars and learned how to make it believable. Our attitude to audiences was 'You will like it'. We didn't need a licence to be a musician. We KNEW it was good."

The album begins with the doomy 'Five Years' in which the alien star Ziggy comes to earth and announces it is dying due to excessive use of mineral resources. In fact there are only five years left before the end, which leaves both older and younger generations in a quandary. Woody's drums set the pace and strings swoon as Bowie/Ziggy ponders the awful fate of the planet and its peoploids.

The documentary style delivery is quite effective if rather overdone as panic spreads, civilisation collapses and black holes from outer space are used by 'The Infinites' to hop around the universe. Ziggy proclaims himself a prophet (rather like Vince Taylor) but the star men tear him apart, a scene fully described in final number 'Rock And Roll Suicide'.

'Soul Love' that follows 'Five Years' is about the various forms of love, whether for a boy for a girl or a priest for the word of God. David adds some saxophone licks that confirm any solo bookings at Ronnie Scott's Club would have been unlikely. The highlight of an otherwise unexceptional performance is the guitar solo from Ronson.

'Moonage Daydream' commences with the announcement "I'm an alligator…I'm a space invader". The song was earlier unveiled on the Arnold Corns version and is intended to represent Ziggy himself in action as a rock 'n' roller although it is more pop than rock. 'Starman' is much better and was already intended to be a single before it was included on the album.

"There's a Starman waiting in the sky, he'd like to come and meet us but he thinks he'd blow our minds" sings David. Ziggy

is supposed to have written the story of the Starman who comes in peace to bring relief and hope to those fearful of the tales of impending doom outlined in 'Five Years'. The song was released as a single in April 1972 and leapt to Number 10 in the UK charts, his first hit since 'Space Oddity'. He needed a boost to his career even at this stage, as he was still playing local gigs for as little as £150 a night. However 'Starman' failed to make an impression in the States – a real oddity.

'It Ain't Easy' that follows is a song credited to American composer Ron Davies that allows Mick Ronson to play some excellent slide guitar and includes some backing vocals from Dana Gillespie. It's back to the Ziggy-o-Sphere with 'Lady Stardust' a soulful and wistful performance by Bowie with strong piano accompaniment, presumably by Ronson. A tribute to Marc Bolan it was originally entitled 'He Was Alright (The Band Was Altogether).'

The next number 'Star' is an up tempo boogie that Elton John might have enjoyed and which imagines Ziggy as a member of the audience deciding whether he could be a star too. The use of the word 'star' crops up in song titles no less than four times throughout the album. Count 'em.

'Hang On To Yourself' sounds like punk rock four years earlier than scheduled, and bounces along with an irresistible lively beat, lots of hand clapping and slide guitar. "We're the Spiders From Mars" is the cry as the band slips and slides towards a fun finale with yells of "Come on" during a finale that owes more to Eddie

Cochran than Lou Reed. As a tribute to a groupie the band sound like they're having a lot of fun and 'Hang On To Yourself' became a perfect opening number for live shows during 1972 and beyond.

Ziggy Stardust commences with Mick Ronson's superb guitar introduction followed by David's proud and slightly nervous proclamation "Ziggy played guitar…" The whole performance sums up the mood and excitement of rock music during a sizzling period, with Bowie making and chronicling his own history even before the media could catch up and comprehend such breathtaking audacity. His evocative lyrics helped define the concept of the ultimate pop star. However it couldn't last and Ziggy would ultimately break up his band – a prophecy that Bowie took seriously.

'Suffragette City' is a rock 'n' roll rave up released as the B-side to 'Starman' and a song supposedly about feminism or least the physical power of the opposite sex. Note his interesting observation: "Hey man, I gotta straighten my face. This mellow thighed chick just put my spine out of place", followed by the breathless exclamation "Wham bam thank you Ma'am". The performance gradually speeds up as the Spiders reach a climax of rock 'n' roll freedom.

'Rock 'n' Roll Suicide' concludes the saga of Ziggy Stardust as his five years on Earth come to an end. It encapsulates Bowie's concept of the rock artist as a shooting star making a meteoric leap across the skies before burning himself out. Bowie was drawn to Pete Townshend's famous line in The Who's classic 'My Generation' when Roger Daltrey sings "I hope I die before I get old". As it turns out most rock stars preferred to carry on rocking well into old age and enjoy every last minute of careers that lasted decades rather than a mere five years.

At the time of course Bowie felt that he'd already discovered all that life had to hold and that only the young deserved to live – and to die. The song provided a perfect closing number for the Spiders live shows and was still being performed well into the mid-Seventies. During this final album track David sings out with almost hysterical conviction "You're not alone…give me your hand you're wonderful", a very useful piece of advice to any impressionable fans and a performance worthy of Judy Garland encouraging the Cowardly Lion in *The Wizard of Oz*. And so it was heigh ho and farewell to Ziggy Stardust. All hail *Aladdin Sane*.

Above left: David Bowie (Ziggy Stardust) kicking his way to stardom, on stage in 1972. But where were the Spiders?...

Right: Bowie, circa 1972, performing on stage dressed as Ziggy Stardust. By the end of July, 1973 Ziggy was no more to be seen.

UNLEASH THE DIAMOND DOGS

In the aftermath of 'Ziggy Stardust' the world was David Bowie's oyster. He could press on with writing, performing and producing more captivating music and even embrace a new career as an actor on stage and in movies. A mesmerizing personality with a gift of metamorphosing into different roles, theatre and cinema seemed obvious new areas to utilize those talents.

Yet despite his popularity and magnetism, it wasn't always a done deal to find the right roles, or even keep up the pace as an innovative musician. Just like many stars before him, he would find that hard-won triumphs in one field didn't guarantee success in another.

It was hard enough to find a successor to Ziggy Stardust as a rock star, let alone conquer new realms in the arts and entertainment. Sometimes he faltered and allowed himself the luxury of falling for the obvious escapes routes into the oblivion that the rock world was only to ready to provide.

At the start of the Seventies there were other obstacles to Bowie's quest for happiness and fulfilment. He began to realize that despite selling many albums and singles and being feted in the media and idolized by fans, he was actually financially broke and still living in a rented flat. Even when he performed at such prestige venues as the Rainbow Theatre in London, it was later revealed that his fees weren't sufficient to pay for extra musicians and guest artists.

There was massive expenditure on Bowie's behalf by his business representatives eager to promote him America, where it was deemed important to look successful and lead the lifestyle of a megastar. The Bowie vision seemed impressive but behind the scenes money from royalties was slow to accrue, not all the shows sold out and ticket sales away from major cities on the first U.S. tour in September 1972 were often very poor. While the entourage was running up hefty hotel bills, the tour wasn't earning enough money to cover such expense and the record company RCA was expected to pick up the tab.

It later transpired that far from becoming rich, Bowie was falling into debt. His musicians weren't being paid much either, which became a cause for unrest and bad feeling backstage. David retreated into his 'Ziggy' persona as if to insulate himself from the stress of touring, putting on exhausting shows and coping with the demands of a media anxious to probe into the depths of the strange new phenomenon from England.

The three Spiders From Mars had been with Bowie since before the start of the 'Ziggy' era. Now they were joined by American keyboard player Mike Garson, a fine musician, who it turned out was being paid considerably more than the rest of the band. The original Spiders had lived through the tough times and felt they deserved better.

Woody Woodmansey: "When we first went out gigging, audiences used to throw beer bottles at us while we were playing. Various objects would come bouncing off my cymbals! It was dangerous, because they'd not seen anything like us before.

"When we got to the States I noticed the press really didn't want to speak to David Jones. They actually wanted to interview Ziggy Stardust. So he would comply with that and *be* that persona. Then it kinda got so he was always Ziggy. I got into a taxi with him one day and asked if he'd seen 'that sci-fi film on TV last night?' Nothing. I thought, did I not speak loud enough? 'Did you see that film David?' Then I realized I was speaking to Ziggy Stardust. So communication got kind of hard. Until then we had always travelled together. Then he started travelling in separate limousines."

Once on stage everything remained happy enough between David and his Spiders. When the ensemble played at Radio City, in New York, the lads noticed there were four trap doors in the stage. They suggested it would be good fun if they all came up through different trap doors. Woody: "When we came up the place went bonkers. But we had just had a fight back stage, probably about a jacket David had wanted me to wear, and I'd said 'no'. Once we got on stage, we just played."

The band had all their expenses paid, but wages remained low and when this was brought to the attention of the management it didn't go down well. When David found out, he wasn't best pleased either. It wasn't long before there was a dramatic parting of the ways and Ziggy himself was consigned to outer space from whence he came.

Woody: "We talked a lot about what we were going to do in the future and David had gone into the soul thing and I didn't like that. I like my music to be based in rock. And then he said he didn't want me to be featured in the shows and that didn't seem so

Previous page: David Bowie in fully Ziggy Stardust persona, live on stage at Earls Court Arena, May 12, 1973, photograph by Gijsbert Hanekroot.

Right: Bare legged, arms akimbo, Bowie struts, pouts and performs in a white kimono. This was worn beneath his original stage costume.

appealing. There were financial things that weren't quite right and also I didn't hit it off with the manager."

Even with such undercurrents developing during the U.S. tour it didn't stop David from writing whenever he could, often in the back seat of a rented Greyhound bus. This was their mode of tour transport as Bowie refused to fly anywhere, his nerves shot after a stormy trip home from a trip to Cyprus with Angela. He'd rather cross the Atlantic by ocean liner and travel to Japan by train across Russia if possible.

He began assembling material for the aptly named *Aladdin Sane* during his hectic travels. Among the new songs was 'The Jean Genie' written in Nashville and quickly recorded in an

RCA studio. This was followed by 'Drive-In Saturday', 'Panic In Detroit' and 'Cracked Actor' all inspired by the stories he heard and people he met and observed on the road. 'The Jean Genie' coupled with 'Ziggy Stardust' was released by RCA in November and the U.S. tour finally finished with concerts in Philadelphia on December 2. Arriving back in London, Bowie performed two special shows at the Rainbow Theatre and more UK concerts took place in January 1973.

Bowiemania reached a peak as 'The Jean Genie' got to Number 2 in the UK chart in December 1972, his third and biggest hit of a year that had seen 'Starman' reaching Number 10 in June and 'John, I'm Only Dancing' a post-Ziggy song at Number 12 in September. During 1973 Bowie bounced back in the UK charts with 'Drive In Saturday' a Number 3 hit in April, 'Life On Mars', a Number 3 smash in June, the reissued 'Laughing Gnome' chuckling back to Number 6 in September and 'Sorrow' peaking at Number 3 in October.

As well as writing and producing his own hits, Bowie had been busy elsewhere helping to launch rock group Mott The Hoople, producing their album and giving them a hit single with *All The*

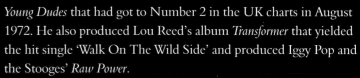

Young Dudes that had got to Number 2 in the UK charts in August 1972. He also produced Lou Reed's album *Transformer* that yielded the hit single 'Walk On The Wild Side' and produced Iggy Pop and the Stooges' *Raw Power*.

It was a punishing schedule and David explained: "When you become well known you' re sure it's only going to last for a limited time so you cram as much work in as possible. I was also writing and working up ideas for future shows before it all disappeared."

In January 1973 Bowie sailed back to New York on board the *QE2* ocean liner for his second tour that began with a show at Radio City Music Hall, where he fainted on stage. He wasn't eating enough and the strain of life as Ziggy was taking its toll. However, he zig-zagged south and west across the States by bus with an expanded band and finished up in Los Angeles with two shows at the Long Beach Auditorium. As well as the Spiders and Mike Garson, the band now included extra drummer Aynsley Dunbar and Ken Fordham on saxophone.

Next came a trip to Japan in April where disappointingly his eight shows were not complete sell-outs. But it was all an adventure including an epic trip back from the east overland by Trans-Siberian express across Russia to Paris and London. During his long absence from England *Aladdin Sane* was released in April 13, 1973. Here at last was the eagerly awaited follow up to *The Rise and Fall Of Ziggy Stardust…* Would Aladdin rise or fall? The answer was swift. The genie rose to the occasion with another highly successful album. Advance orders of 100,000 ensuring it shot up to Number One in the charts. In May the star embarked on another major tour with 27 concerts at home, beginning with a show at London's Earls Court on May 12.

This cavernous hall normally reserved for exhibitions, proved unsuitable for a sophisticated rock concert. It was the era before PA systems were properly developed and there was trouble in store. The show had sold out and 18,000 fans converged on the West London venue. However they found it hard to see and hear the show properly and with gangs of visiting Australian youths misbehaving rather than only dancing in the aisles, Bowie angrily cancelled the next day's concert to avoid further chaos.

Thankfully the UK tour continued with sold-out shows guaranteed around the country, unlike in America where despite his high media profile, record and ticket sales failed to match expectations. He still had yet to gain a Top Ten US hit, although 'Space Oddity' had finally reached Number 15 in *Billboard* in February 1973. Another proposed US was put into touch and in a neat manoeuvre it was announced that David would retire from live appearances due to "exhaustion".

The shock news broke at London's Odeon Hammersmith on July 3, 1973 towards the end of a show filmed by D.A.Pennebaker,

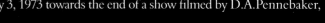

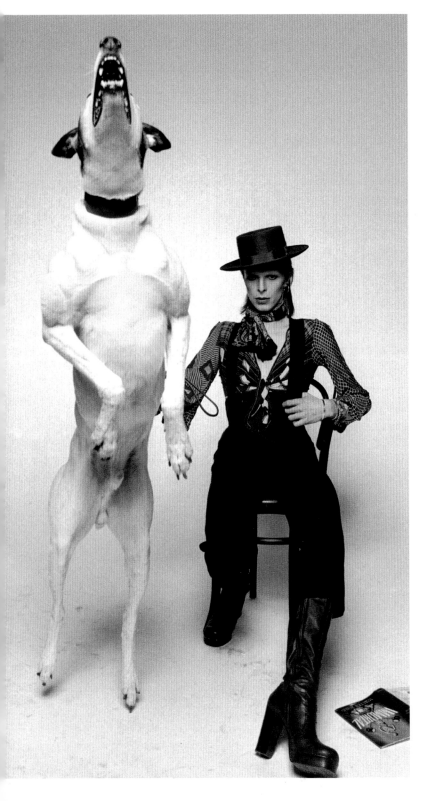

D.A.Pennebaker, famed for his 1967 Bob Dylan documentary *Don't Look Back*. It seems only Mick Ronson knew that the show would be the last performance by the Spiders From Mars. It was certainly a shock for Woody Woodmansey and Trevor Bolder – not to mention the audience.

After performing songs from 'Ziggy Stardust' and a string of hits including 'The Jean Genie' when Jeff Beck joined Mick Ronson in a jam on stage, David announced: "This show will stay the longest in our memories, not just because it is the end of the tour but because it's the last show we'll ever do…" He then sang 'Rock 'n' Roll Suicide' while the audience succumbed to tears and screams of "No!" Band members Trevor and Woody were equally confused as it was all news to them. They were convinced they were about to go on another American tour. Now they realized, they had been sacked. The Spiders From Mars and Ziggy Stardust were no more.

The news caused a sensation as it was revealed Bowie and his management had turned down an apparently lucrative 80-date US tour. A star-studded farewell party was thrown at London's Café Royal where David explained to friends Mick Jagger and Lou Reed that he needed to 'retire' from Ziggy and rock 'n' roll to try new things that would acting in movies. His next move was study various film scripts, reevaluate his life and recover from Ziggy, the proto-rock 'n' roll star he had created and that had come to life like Frankenstein's monster. Sadly the monster had to die.

Said David: "People treated me as they would have treated Ziggy. I became convinced I was the next Messiah. I fell for Ziggy too. I got hopelessly lost in the fantasy and the concerts especially in America got enormously frightening."

All was not lost to distraught Bowie fans. *Aladdin Sane*, with its striking gatefold LP cover, retained the power to shock and delight. It depicted a red haired Bowie with a scarlet lightning flash across his forehead and right eye, a spectacle that became an iconic image of the Seventies. Inside the sleeve was a picture of David naked with his modesty covered in silver spray paint.

The music was equally challenging and emotive. There was less emphasis on the guitar work of Mick Ronson, (who Bowie's management was promising to launch as a solo artist) and more focus on Mike Garson's piano playing. Nevertheless the record came to be seen as the last hurrah for Glam Rock as a creative force and not just another pop fashion trend.

Previous pages: Ziggy Stardust plays the Radio City Music Hall in New York, USA on February 14, 1973. Photograph by Neal Preston.

Above: The post-Ziggy Stardust David Bowie posing with a large dog, working on the cover of the 1974 album *Diamond Dogs*.

Right: David on the road. The Ziggy Stardust World Tour of 1973. It started in Scotland and took in the UK, USA and Japan, and culimated in London.

The songs on *Aladdin Sane* mostly summed up his experiences on tour in the States where the air of frenzied decadence was ultimately sapping both his strength and morale. Bowie: "Aladdin was really Ziggy in America. I met some very mixed-up people and got very upset which resulted in "Aladdin". I knew then I didn't have much more to say about rock 'n' roll." He added: "I don't think Aladdin was as clear cut and defined a character as Ziggy."

Opening cut 'Watch That Man' is predicated on a good old USA boogie rock riff with strong bass playing and excellent guitar. David tells how "Shakey threw a party that lasted all night". It seems everybody drank a lot of "something nice" there was an "old fashioned band" and "the ladies looked fab".

'Aladdin Sane (1913-1938-197?)' summons images of Aladdin and His Magic Lamp, a stalwart of Christmas pantomime shows. But 'a lad insane' heralds a piece full of gloomy thoughts about doom and destruction. Garson's piano proffers rhapsodic chords and trills to complement Ronson's surging guitar as David sings with greater clarity than on the previous rave up. He explores his vocal range on a theatrical piece Ziggy fans would no doubt find hard to take on board, but it certainly creates an air of insanity.

'Drive-In Saturday' was a UK single but failed to chart in the US, even though the composer saw it as one of his more commercial offerings. Written on the band bus travelling between Seattle and Phoenix it was inspired by the sight of a row of radar domes designed to give early warning of a nuclear attack. David images a future when radiation has neutralized the human race's sex life and they are reduced to watching movies about love making at drive-in cinemas.

'Panic In Detroit' was written in Los Angeles after a night out with Iggy Pop and is concerned with the ultimate failure of urban revolution while Bowie himself is torn between anti-materialism and riches. Apart from an insistent Bo Diddley beat it loses direction in a traffic jam of noise.

Previous page: David Bowie on stage with the Spiders From Mars in 1973. That year they toured the world before Ziggy called time in July.
Above: David's last television appearance as Ziggy Stardust – on NBC's *The Midnight Special* in 1973.

Right: David, photographed by Mick Rock, in Chicago, Ill, USA in October 1972. He would be back in the USA only a few months later as part of the Ziggy Stardust and the Spiders From Mars tour of 1973.

'Cracked Actor' was written during a stay at the Beverley Hills Hotel in Los Angeles and is a vision of him as a mature film star in the future on hard times and cruising in search of sleazy sex. 'Time' is a Berlin-in-the-1930s cabaret style indulgence that contains the memorable line "flexes like a whore, falls wanking to the floor" that drew a shocked reaction whenever performed in public. The song deals with the ravages of time and its effect on the once beautiful and famous. Garson and Ronson do sterling service in conjuring up a suitably dramatic, camp atmosphere.

'The Prettiest Star' is back on safer ground as a hand clapping reprise of the song that first appeared as a single in 1970 with

Marc Bolan on guitar guesting with Bowie's then band Hype. The song is about Angela Barnett and not Bolan. The main riff drags along in uninspired fashion but matters improve with the band's launch into a spirited version of the Rolling Stones' 'Let's Spend The Night Together'. Mick Jagger and Bowie were hanging out together at the time this was recorded and the unequivocal message "let's make love" makes a change from the oblique and convoluted angst of much of *Aladdin Sane*.

'The Jean Genie' is one of the best tracks on the album and one of Bowie's greatest hits. It's simplistic R&B beat harks back to the King Bees and his teenage year, while the 'talking blues' style deliver is a welcome return to vocal clarity. 'The Jean Genie' is supposedly a tribute to Iggy Pop while it can also be seen as a reference to notorious French author Jean Genet who scandalized society with his novel *Our Lady Of The Flowers*, a portrayal of crime, sex and violence.

Mike Garson is in best Liberace mode for 'Lady Grinning Soul' as his piano accompanies la Bowie making a grand entrance with an extravagant and romantic ballad that celebrates the delights of anticipated love making. A sparkling performance shows David

Left: Portrait of David Bowie in the USA, circa February 1973. **Above:** Backstage with Bowie. A moment of rare calm for David/Ziggy before the concert begins. **Above right:** An entire team was dedicated to preparing Bowie and his

many costumes for concerts. **Overleaf:** David Bowie and Spiders' guitarist Mick Ronson dining on a train on their way to Aberdeen, Scotland for a concert in May 1973. Photographed by Mick Rock.

at his best as a vocalist of style and distinction blessed with a remarkable range, sense of timing and pitch.

Bowie's next album would continue the trend set by 'Let's Spend The Night Together'. *Pin Ups*, released in October 1973, spared the world another Ziggy-like creation and instead celebrated all the great British hits by everyone's favourite Sixties groups. It came at a time when progression was all the rage, but Bowie cried "halt" and overnight retro became cool. He achieved this by assembling an excellent selection of cover versions.

The band was reinvigorated by the arrival of drummer Aynsley Dunbar who made his presence felt on The Who songs 'I Can't Explain' and 'Anyway, Anyhow, Anywhere' and on the Pink Floyd classic 'See Emily Play'. Other covers included The Pretty Things' 'Rosalyn', 'Here Comes The Night', a hit for Van Morrison and Them, 'I Wish You Would' and 'Shapes Of Things' by The Yardbirds, 'Everything's Alright' by The Mojos, 'Friday On My Mind' by the Easybeats, 'Sorrow' by The Merseys, 'Don't Bring Me Down' a hit for The Animals, and The Kinks' 'Where Have All The Good Times Gone'.

Pin Ups proved hugely popular, went straight to Number one and sold 30,000 copies a week, ensuring it stayed in the charts for five months. The string-laden Bowie cover of 'Sorrow'

that had been a Number 4 hit for The Merseys in 1966, got to Number 3 in October 1973.

Pin Ups, with its delightful cover shot showing Bowie and supermodel soul mate Twiggy clad in a body stocking represented a celebration of Bowie's past when pop was a happier, more innocent place. He described the album himself as "A pleasure. And I knew the band was over. It was a last farewell to them."

Looming over the postwar generation alongside the threat of nuclear war was the ominous vision of a totalitarian future as described in George Orwell's 1948 novel *1984*. Hailed now as one of the greatest books in the English language, it imagines a Britain ruled as a one party state fronted by Big Brother, the revered leader.

Above: Preparing to take the stage as Ziggy Stardust. Pierre La Roche was David's make-up artist.

Right: David Bowie holding *Hunky Dory* under his arm. This pre-punk version of Bowie was photographed by Mick Rock in London in 1972.

Under its laws every thought and deed is controlled and enforced by a ubiquitous network of telescreens, a two-way surveillance device installed in the streets and in party member's apartments. Relentless propaganda and cruel torture are used to bend the will of the people into subservience. It is an austere world of permanent war, "hate weeks", "doublethink" and "thought police."

The book caused a sensation on publication and became even more widely known when adapted as a play by BBC TV, a production that caused widespread alarm and controversy when televised in 1954. The actor Peter Cushing won praise for his role as the hero/victim Winston Smith. The chilling phrase "Orwellian future" became commonplace and many genuinely feared the arrival of the year 1984 and the possibility that Orwell's predictions might come true.

All this impressed David Bowie in his youth and nurtured a desire to devise a full-scale musical based on the book with him playing the role of Winston Smith. He began writing songs for his *1984* during a stay in a villa in Rome after the success of *Pin Ups*. However, his scheme had to be curtailed when Orwell's widow refused him permission to base a musical on her husband's work.

With the songs all ready he now had to create his own vision of a dystopian future called Hunger City that became the basis of his next album, *Diamond Dogs*. The story was set in a post-nuclear holocaust land where sub-human "Peoploids" roam the streets looting shops and surrounded by rabid dogs and mutant rats.

Although the subsequent album lacked a coherent narrative many of the songs referred directly to Orwell's vision including 'We Are The Dead', '1984' and 'Big Brother Chant Of The Ever Circling Skeletal Family'. The album was recorded in London and Hilversum during January and February 1974 with assistance from Tony Visconti providing string arrangements and a band of session men, Tony Newman and Aynsley Dunbar on drums, Herbie Flowers on bass and Mike Garson on keyboards. With Mick Ronson busy launching his solo career, Bowie played lead guitar himself.

Diamond Dogs (RCA) was released April 24, 1974 and the LP came resplendent in a gatefold sleeve with a disturbing cover painting by Guy Peelaert depicting Bowie as half man and half

dog. The original sleeve showed the creature's sex organs, which was way too offensive for the record company. The first batch of albums was recalled and the artwork airbrushed in the interests of public decency. Even then it wasn't one of Bowie's most attractive album covers and the music didn't impress the critics much either even though it yielded at least two major hit singles.

David later confessed he wasn't a great fan of *Diamond Dogs* and explained that he wasn't really a fan of the concept album and that there was a deal of tension around the making of the record. "I had done so much of it myself. It was frightening trying to make an album with no support and I was very much on my own. It was a relief that it did so well."

Despite its gloomy theme, unprepossessing cover and backlash from critics who described the songs as "mediocre" *Diamond*

Previous pages, left: David Bowie in Newcastle City Hall playing one of the first concerts on the Ziggy Stardust tour of 1973. **Previous pages, right:** David on stage again, at the Earls Court Arena on May 12, 1973. Photograph by Gijsbert Hanekroot.

Left: David Bowie with his wife Angie Bowie, photographed outside the Café Royal in Regents Street, London in July 1973. Bowie hosted what became known as the 'Last Supper' as he and a group of friends bid farewell to Ziggy Stardust for the last time.

Above: Bowie, wearing an eye patch, conducts a press conference at the Amstel Hotel in Amsterdam, Holland on February 13, 1974. Photographed by Gijsbert Hanekroot. His follow-up to Ziggy Stardust – the *Diamond Dogs* tour – was yet to begin.

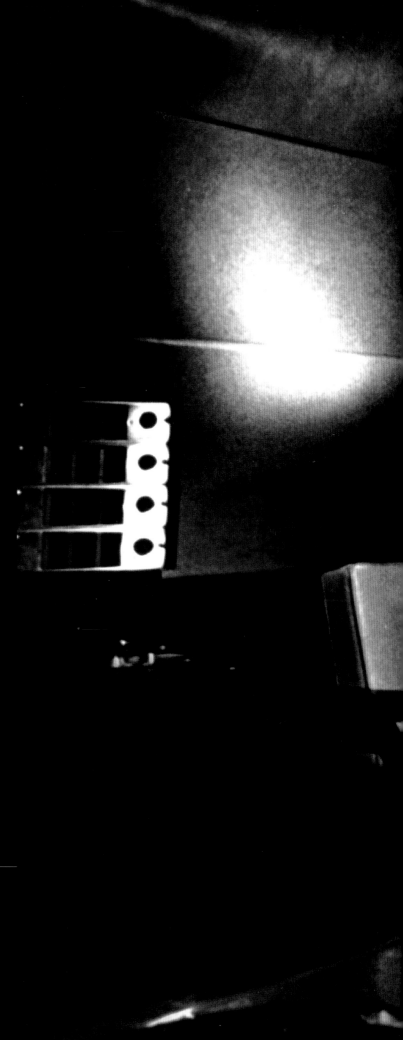

Dogs was a best seller and became the basis for a massive North American tour intended to be the most spectacular rock shows ever staged. Ironically while rehearsing his band for two months in New York in April 1974, Bowie found himself listening to black soul music at the Apollo Theatre in Harlem that would help determine his next change of musical direction.

The Diamond Dogs Revue opened at the Montreal Forum in Canada on June 14 and featured a one and a half hour show with a specially designed stage set filled with dancers, special lighting effects and machinery. It was like a Broadway show with props that included a 20-foot high catwalk for *Bowie* as he was now billed.

The aim was to create Hunger City, a decadent metropolis with Bowie acting out the various characters. Ziggy Stardust was banished and Bowie now performed wearing a light grey suit and white shirt. The show was widely praised, even by critics who weren't thrilled by the album.

It all reached a climax with a show at Madison Square Garden on July 19, 1974 when the songs performed included '1984', 'Rebel

Above: Starman: Bowie, on acoustic guitar, plays one of his most famous tunes at the Hammersmith Odeon in July 1973 – Ziggy's 'farewell concert.'

Right: A much more casual looking David Bowie in the studio recording the *Diamond Dogs* album. Work was split between London and Amsterdam.

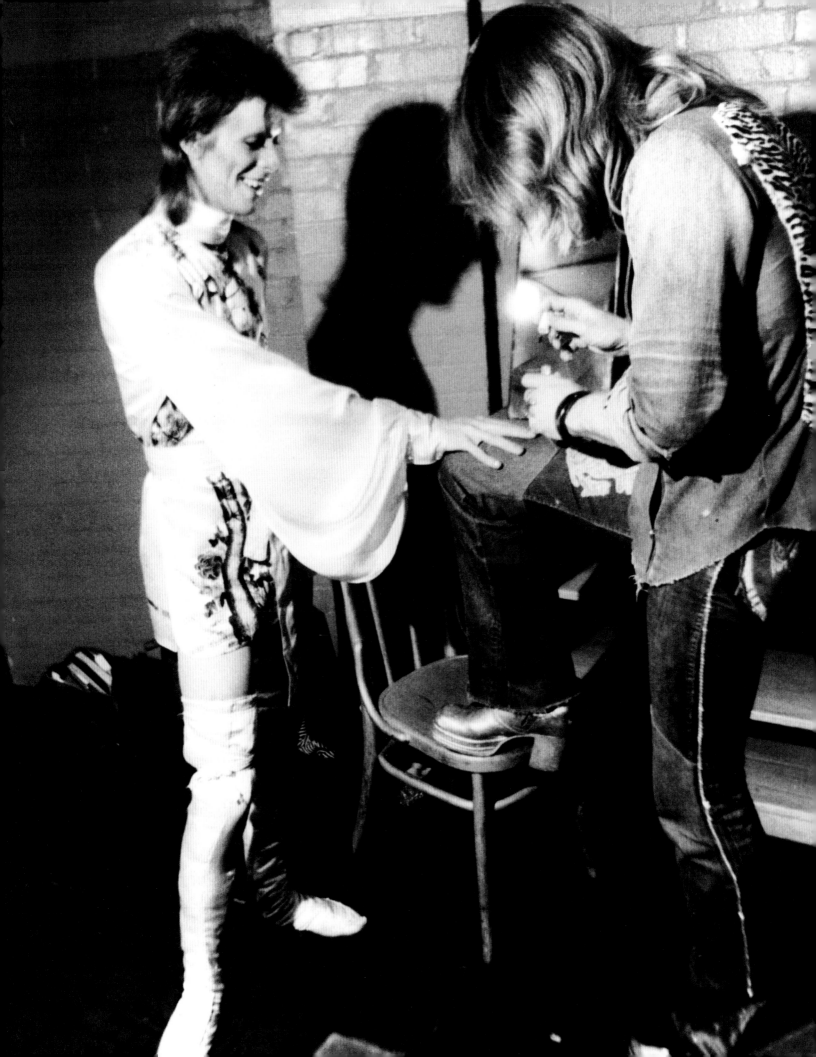

Rebel', 'All The Young Dudes' and even 'Space Oddity'. The show was also recorded for the *David Live* album at the Tower Theatre, Philadelphia on July 14 and 15. More US touring followed but it was deemed too expensive to be staged back home in Britain.

Diamond Dogs begins with the howling horrors of Hunger City as David narrates in sepulchre tones the scene setting 'Future Legend'. He describes fleas the size of rats and rats the size of cats and ten thousand peoploids with mutant red eyes dividing into groups as they await the year of the Diamond Dogs. Unfortunately it sounds more Spinal Tap than George Orwell, but Bowie's well-known sense of humour may have been bubbling under the surface.

The title track kicks off with out of tune guitar lending a suitably decadent tone. Released as a single in June 1974 it got to Number 21 in the UK charts. But the best and biggest hit track is 'Rebel Rebel' that tells the story of a tomboy rock chick who has torn her dress and whose face "is a mess". Complete with memorable Stones-style guitar riff supplied by a guest session player Alan Parker, 'Rebel Rebel' enlivened an otherwise gloomy album and shot to Number 5 in the UK in February 1974.

Among the other tracks 'Rock 'n' Roll With Me' is a slow piece with piano and organ adding a touch of gospel soul backing to Bowie's overwrought vocals. 'We Are The Dead' is a phrase used by Winston Smith and his lover when they are unmasked by prying telescreens and Bowie intones the lyrics with restrained sincerity. '1984' is a string laden disco theme that hints at Bowie's own more soul future and was also covered by Tina Turner on her 1984 album *Private Dancer*. 'Big Brother' deals with the leader of "Airstrip One", as Britain has now become. His image on huge posters glare down on the populace demanding eternal love and loyalty. The songs that leads into the 'Chant Of The Ever Circling Skeletal Family', a tape loop that concludes the album.

Whatever the weaknesses of *Diamond Dogs* it helped sustain the image of Bowie as bold experimentalist who could also be relied on to pluck magical chart hits from the air. The Thin White Duke was about to appear and conquer yet more worlds.

Left: Make-up artist Pierre La Roche prepares David Bowie for a performance as 'Aladdin Sane' rather than Ziggy Stardust. Bowie's costume is by Japanese designer Kansai Yamamoto.

Right above: David Bowie and close friend Lou Reed. The two have worked together many times.
Right: Ziggy Stardust and a Spider From Mars – David Bowie and guitarist Mick Ronson in Manchester, 1973.

MOVIES & DUETS

David Bowie had seemed adrift in pop space until Major Tom came floating into his life. The late Sixties proved a frustrating period for him in some respects. Yet that didn't stop the artist experimenting, seeking new ideas and gaining valuable experience.

At the time he began filming, Bowie was entering his 'Thin White Duke' period, and drawing away from rock and getting into disco and soul music. Under extreme personal pressures, his personality changed and he now emanated an air of loneliness and alienation. The once cheery 'London boy' now seemed cold and emotionless, a man with the fixed expression of a sad-faced mime artist. Ironically this proved entirely appropriate for his most challenging acting assignment.

Meanwhile, his departure from the joys of Glam Rock was marked by the 1975 album *Young Americans*. A smart, clean cut Bowie appears on the album cover complete with coiffured hair, gold bangles and a smart check shirt. A photograph, taken for the sleeve by Eric Stephen Jacobs, captured his mood and confirmed the demise of Ziggy and Aladdin Sane.

It was one of a number of crucial changes in his life that saw the ending of important relationships; first with the Spiders From Mars and then his wife Angela, manager Tony Defries and management company Mainman. Henceforth he would take charge of his own business affairs. He was determined to join the ranks of the superstars rather than remain among the poor relations.

In between *Diamond Dogs* and *Young Americans* came *David Live*, a double LP set that had been recorded in Philadelphia during the 1974 *Diamond Dogs* US tour.

Although Bowie was accompanied by a slick band with David Sanborn on saxophone and Earl Slick on guitar, the overall sound was flat and critics deemed the performances lifeless. The cover also showed an incredibly thin Bowie in a blue suit with high-waisted trousers, wearing an expression of extreme pain. Bowie himself later commented that the photographs made him look "As if I've just stepped out of the grave". However, the record did yield a surprise hit with a stirring version of Eddie Floyd's 'Knock On Wood', a soul classic that got to Number 10 in the UK.

More hits followed when the single 'Young Americans' got to 17 in the UK in March 1975. It was his second US chart entry that got to Number 28 in *Billboard* in April following the belated success of 'Space Oddity' in February that year. But there was real joy when David Bowie scored his first Number One in America with the hypnotic 'Fame' that leapt into the chart in August.

'Fame' marked an historic moment when David worked with his Beatles idol John Lennon, who co-wrote the song and also sang on the track. John also played on Bowie's cover of the Lennon and McCartney number 'Across The Universe'.

David had first met Lennon at a party in Beverly Hills hosted by Elizabeth Taylor in the summer of 1974. They got on well and Lennon offered Bowie advice on business and management matters. They met up again in New York in January 1975 and recorded 'Fame' at the Electric Lady Studio with former Jimi Hendrix engineer Eddie Kramer. Most of the new material was written in the studio with the aim of appealing directly to, naturally enough, young Americans.

Although Bowie himself later referred to the music as "plastic soul" it achieved the desired effect and the relative simplicity of the concept helped him through a difficult and traumatic period.

The title track has wailing saxophone, a lilting beat and attractive melody. Bowie adopts a breathless, rap style over a groove inspired by visits to New York and LA clubs and discos. It was an experience that made him realise youth culture was moving away from rock and into dance music. David: "Hanging around the clubs I began to feel the new disco thing. I just got caught up in the mood and crammed my whole American experience into the song."

Among the other album tracks 'Win' is a gentle ballad that surges like the sea. The singer hopes people realize that behind the Bowie facade is a real flesh and blood human being. It was one of his favourite tracks. The next item 'Fascination' was co-written with singer/songwriter Luther Vandross, then working as one of Bowie's backing soul singers. Carlos Alomar provides the funky wah wah guitar and sexy backing vocalists help the lead singer whip up a creamy climax.

'Right' is based on a simple guitar riff behind a chant of "Never no turning back". Recorded in Philadelphia and honouring the famed 'Philly Sound' it is intended to be a drone style erotic vibration with universal appeal.

Previous page: David Bowie in Munich, Germany in 1976. The extravagant glam rock fashion of Ziggy is long forgotten: enter the Thin White Duke.

Right: David Bowie drew much critical praise for his role as Joseph Merrick in *The Elephant Man* on Broadway, New York 1980.

Left: Always keen to explore visual as well as musical and performing arts, David Bowie in Los Angeles, California, USA in 1976.

Above: David Bowie was always sharply dressed, as this 1974 photograph by Terry O'Neill shows. Note the contrasting coloured hair.

On 'Somebody Up There Likes Me' Bowie warns about the dangers of the cult of personality amidst a slow drag tune enlivened by saxophones and strings. The title was inspired by the 1956 movie starring Paul Newman and featuring Sal Mineo.

After his Philly sessions, Bowie moved to the Record Plant in New York to mix the tracks. There he cut his version of 'Across The Universe' a song from The Beatles' 1970 *Let It Be* album. Bowie's new mate John Lennon came into the studio and he sings on the track with David who performs in rather strange fashion, becoming increasingly manic like a pantomime villain: "Nothing's gonna change my world!"

'Can You Hear Me' is another Philly track that begins sadly

'Once we were lovers' and is a message to … one of his lovers. A slow ballad with strings Bowie sings normally most of the way but suddenly drops into a peculiar tonal effect rather like Buddy Holly on a night out with Lonnie Donegan, before escalating up into a falsetto stratosphere.

'Fame' comes as a joyful relief after this indulgence, with Bowie getting into a groove with help from John Lennon and Carlos Alomar. Added as an afterthought to the album it became one of Bowie's biggest hits. Born out of a studio jam the simple chant of 'Fame!' was a mantra about Lennon and Bowie's shared life experiences and the guitar riff was courtesy of Carlos Alomar. It was Lennon who encouraged Bowie to turn the jam into a full blown track, proclaiming all that was needed to get a hit single was the right hook and a solid beat. Together they achieved victory on all fronts.

After *Young Americans* succeeded in helping Bowie finally crack the States, 'The Thin White Duke' era was epitomized by Bowie's next studio album *Station To Station*. This was written and recorded while still living in Los Angeles. But first he had to concentrate

Left: David Bowie in New York, NY, USA in 1974. The newspaper's original caption read 'In a recent poll, Bowie was voted both the No. 3 male vocalist and the No. 1 female vocalist.'

Above: David Bowie with celebrated French actress Catherine Deneuve on the set of vampire movie *The Hunger*, in 1983. The film was directed by Tony Scott.

on filming *The Man Who Fell To Earth*. Work began with director Nicholas Roeg on location in the deserts around Lake Fenton, New Mexico during July and August 1975.

Bowie was a keen film fan, particularly interested in expressionist movies. He had already tried and failed to launch his own film projects based on the *Ziggy Stardust* and *Diamond Dogs* albums. The Nicolas Roeg film seemed a perfect project for him. The screenplay was a based on a 1963 novel by William Tevis and originally both Peter O'Toole and actor/author Michael Crichton were considered to play the role of an extra-terrestrial that had crashed landed on Earth.

However Roeg had been intrigued by Bowie's appearance in the BBC TV documentary *Cracked Actor* and knew that the star had experience as a mime artist. Bowie was shorter stature than the alien Newton as described in the book, but he had the disconcerting manner and 'weird' stare one might expect from an unearthly being. Roeg had worked with a pop star turned actor before when he cast Mick Jagger in 1970's *Performance* and so Bowie became the front runner to play Thomas Newton.

Bowie would confess he was in a fragile state of mind when filming began and didn't fully understand what was going on, in terms of the production process. Yet he threw himself into the role, learned his lines and became as alienated as the character he was

playing. "It was a pretty natural performance," he said later, "and I was eager to please."

The film version of the novel told how the alien Newton had come by space ship from the drought stricken planet Anthea and crash landed in New Mexico. His aim was to raise funds to build a new space vehicle that could ship him home. Thomas looked passably like a human being and used his superior intelligence and technology to set up a huge corporation based on a raft of patented inventions. While earning vast sums of money and becoming extremely rich he encounters an Earth girl called Mary-Lou. They begin a relationship and she introduces the alien to the delights of sex and alcohol. The visitor is seduced and corrupted by modern day society. Meanwhile, suspicions are aroused by his strange demeanour and he is secretly filmed with an X-ray camera by a colleague that reveals his true alien origins. His girlfriend too is of course horrified when she sees through him.

Above: David Bowie in the fantasy movie *Labyrinth*. Although directed by Jim Henson (of *Muppets* fame) and produced by George Lucas (*Star Wars*) it was not an instant hit.

Above and left: Bowie's differing performances: as Andy Warhol in *Basquiat*, 1993; on stage with Marianne Faithfull, singing 'I Got You Babe', 1973.

Above: Classic portrait of David Bowie in 1974. Photographed by

Right: David Bowie sings in a recording studio, circa 1975.

Overleaf: Behind the scenes at the 1975 Grammy Awards at New York's

Before Newton can launch his space ship and head back to Anthea he is captured by Government spies and imprisoned. By now addicted to alcohol and reduced to watching endless junk television on a multitude of screens, the broken Newton, finally breaks free from his prison, only to die a drunken, lonely death having failed in his quest.

Reviews for the film when it was finally released in 1976 were mixed. One critic called it "preposterous and posturing" while another said it was "absorbing and beautiful". Bowie won a Saturn Award as Best Actor and *The Man Who Fell To Earth* has since been proclaimed a sci-fi classic. In the aftermath of the film Bowie maintained his appearance as the expressionless alien and even took with him the clothes he wore on set and sported the same haircut. Aladdin Sane was now replaced by The Thin White Duke.

During the late Seventies Bowie maintained a phenomenal workload, making important albums, notably *Station To Station* (1976), *Low* (1977), *"Heroes"* (1977) and *Lodger* (1979) all the while touring and developing his acting experience.

In 1980 David fulfilled one of his ambitions when he starred in a serious play on Broadway. His starring role in the New York production of *The Elephant Man* won him many plaudits and laudatory reviews for an outstanding performance in a difficult role. *The Elephant Man* concerned the real life story of John Merrick who was born in South London in the 1860s and suffered from terrible deformity and disability. He was rescued by a caring doctor from a carnival freak show and eventually accepted into Victorian society as a result of his obvious wit and intelligence.

A play about his life was written by Bernard Pomerance and first performed in London in 1977. When Bowie took the role for an American production in July 1980, he made his debut in Denver followed by seasons in Chicago and New York where the show ended on Broadway in January 1981. David gave a remarkable performance in which he used his skills a mime artist to convey the impression of deformity, rather than resort to using make up or prosthetics. His skill at contortion was physically demanding and even the stage hands were reported to have applauded him at one rehearsal. Bowie was particularly honoured to have appeared on New York's 'Great White Way' which he described as "The biggest single challenge of my career. Going onto Broadway is the fulfilment of a great dream."

David's Elephant Man was acclaimed by theatre critics who said his work was "Shockingly good" and that he was a "True actor who commanded the stage".

More film roles followed including a part in *Just A Gigolo* (1978) filmed in Berlin with Marlene Dietrich and *Merry Christmas Mr. Lawrence* (1983) in which Bowie played Major Jack 'Strafer' Celliers. The film was directed by Nagisma Oshima who had seen Bowie in *The Elephant Man* and had been greatly impressed by his mesmeric presence.

Bowie joined co-star Tom Conti in a movie based on Lawrence van der Post's experiences during the Second World War in a Japanese prisoner of war camp. Bowie plays a soldier who witnessed great cruelty and yet remains spirited and rebellious. He felt that his performance was "The most credible" that he'd done in a film thus far.

In another important role David starred as Jareth the Goblin King in elaborate fantasy epic *Labyrinth* (1986) directed by the late Jim Henson of 'Muppets' fame and produced by *Star Wars* founder George Lucas. The story was based on a quest to reach the centre of a vast maze to rescue a child captured by the Goblin king, with many of the characters played by Jim Henson's puppets.

Bowie was able to help with the script writing and music and liked the idea of it appealing to children "of all ages". He recorded five songs including 'Underground', 'Magic Dance', 'Chilly Down', 'As The World Falls Down' and 'Within You'.

With a budget of $25 million, the complex task of filming began at Elstree Studios in England in April 1985 and took five months to complete. It involved building a huge stage and combining action with puppets, animatronics and live actors. Bowie admitted that interacting with the puppets was a difficult task.

Prince Charles and Princess Diana attended a gala Royal Premiere of *Labyrinth* in London on December 1, 1986. Despite the presence of Bowie as a star attraction, the ambitious film proved a commercial failure at the box office, much to the distress of its creator Jim Henson, who never made another full scale film and died in 1990. It eventually won greater popularity and recognition among film aficionados and has been released on DVD and Blu-ray disc.

In one of his most controversial roles David played Pontius Pilate in *The Last Temptation of Christ*, the fictionalized religious movie directed by Martin Scorsese and shot in Morocco. It was a role that had already been turned down by Gordon 'Sting' Sumner. As Pontius Pilate, Bowie had to denounce Jesus as a threat to the power of the Roman Empire, which led to the Messiah being crowned with thorns and crucified. The completed film was greeted by protests and boycotts mainly due to the suggestion that Jesus was tempted into sexual encounters.

As well as doing a plethora of voiceovers, there were a role in *Absolute Beginners* (1986) the movie based on the 1959 book by Colin MacInnes about life in Fifties London. David composed and performed the movie's theme song that was released as a single in March 1986 together with *Absolute Beginners: The Original Motion Picture Soundtrack* album. Although the film was not well received by the critics, Bowie's single proved a Number Two hit.

He had a cameo role in the David Lynch film *Twin Peaks: Fire Walk With Me* (1991) and Bowie portrayed his old hero Andy Warhol in *Basquiat* (1996). He played himself in *Zoolander* (2001) and was inventor Nikolas Tesla in *The Prestige* (2006).

In January 1976 Bowie released *Station To Station*, expounding on the 'Thin White Duke' image in which his movie persona matched his musical aspirations. After filming *The Man Who Fell To Earth* he admitted he had begun to act like an alien in real life. "I was Newton for six months" he confessed.

While living in Los Angeles he reportedly became obsessed with mysticism, magic, religion and totalitarian political ideas. Bowie seemed to have lost his grip on reality, but had too much talent and intelligence to founder and duty called. Eventually he would escape from LA and relocate to the calmer and tax-friendly environs of Switzerland.

First he went to Cherokee Studios in Hollywood where he began working once again with musicians from the *Young Americans* album, Carlos Alomar and Earl Slick together with Roy Bittan from Bruce Springsteen's E Street Band on keyboards. They evolved a mixture of European and American influences blended with electronica and disco. The title track begins with mind blowing special effects, like an electronic steam train heading down the tracks. A grinding beat develops amongst the keyboards, guitars and drums.

Bowie delays his arrival then announces "The return of the Thin White Duke throwing darts in lovers eyes…" The message of the song may be interpreted in different ways. It could be a religious reference to the Stations of the Cross or simply about his own journeys across America and back to Europe. Bowie was never keen on explaining his lyrics: "People must take what they can from it and see if the information they've assembled fits in with anything I've assembled."

The piece moves on from its mysterious introduction, morphing into an urgent mix of rock and disco, the guitar licks underpinned by a four on the floor dance hall stomp. Bowie's lyrics are barely discernible in the mix apart from the repetitive cry of "Too late".

Previous pages, left: The Thin White Duke on stage. David Bowie performs at Wembley Empire Pool on the *Station To Station* world tour of 1976.

Previous pages, right above: David Bowie on stage with his band at the LA Forum in California in 1976. Note Carlos Alomar on guitar (left).

Previous pages, right below: (left to right) Robert Fripp, David Bowie and Brian Eno at the Hansa Tonstudio, Berlin, Germany, recording *"Heroes"*.

Right: A portrait from 1976, the year *Station To Station* was released. Cameron Crowe described him as a "smartly conservative entertainer."

'Golden Years', a love song written with Angela Bowie in mind, was the only hit single from the album and his first since 'Fame'. It got to Number 8 in the UK after entering the chart in November 1975 and reached Number 10 in the US in January 1976.

Similar to 'Fame' in terms of in its hypnotic beat and riffy echoing vocals, it has undertones of Stevie Wonder's 'Superstition'. Interestingly, the song was offered to Elvis Presley, who turned it down. 'Word On A Wing' is about Bowie's increasing interest in religion as a means of salvation. Roy Bittan's piano urges him on to fresh heights of vocal ecstasy. On 'TVC15' the composer uses the 'cut-up' techniques used by sci-fi author William Burroughs to reduce the power of words and liberate true feelings. It's inspired by the notion of a TV set eating his girlfriend and has an odd but intriguing mix of New Orleans style boogie piano and more modern effects.

On 'Stay' the band to sets up a funky rhythm while Bowie lets them jam a while before talking about the problem of knowing when somebody wants to go – or stay. Excellent guitar work injects much needed musical interplay. But when released as a single, 'Stay' failed to dent the charts.

The sixth and final track 'Wild Is The Wind' is a sad and bleak ballad, written by Dimitri Tiomkin and Ned Washington for the 1957 movie *Wild Is The Wind*, starring Anthony Quinn and originally recorded by Johnny Mathis. It is interpreted with touching tenderness or overwrought exaggeration, depending on one's point of view. With this performance Bowie bid farewell to America and the team of musicians he had worked with for some years.

But not before he embarked on the *Station To Station* World Tour that opened in Vancouver, Canada on February 2, 1976. Gone were the feathers and make up. Bowie appeared clad in black trousers and waistcoat and a plain white shirt and he used minimal stage props and musicians. The days of reckless

Above: David Bowie and Mick Jagger, both looking youthful and happy, in 1987. The lads from south London have worked together occasionally.

Right: A suave-looking David Bowie on stage during the 1974 *Diamond Dogs* tour. When dressed like this it was hard to imagine the same person was Ziggy.

extravagance were over now Bowie was controlling the purse strings. The U.S. dates climaxed with a show at New York's Madison Square Garden on March 26.

David travelled by ship to Europe for concerts in Germany that included a visit to Berlin where he visited the bunker that had been the scene of Hitler's suicide in 1945. He also went to Zurich to see his new Swiss home, set up for him by Angela, where his possessions including books, clothes, antiques and musical instruments had been delivered from America. The tour dates resumed and David's travels took him to Moscow, travelling with his friend Iggy Pop for sight-seeing and shopping.

He arrived back in London in May 1976 ready to promote an album of his greatest hits called *Changesonebowie* (RCA) amidst a press furore over alleged comments he'd made in an interview about fascism that he subsequently denied. That month he performed for six nights at the Empire Pool, Wembley (now the Wembley Arena) then produced *The Idiot* album for Iggy Pop in France, co-writing the songs and playing saxophone and guitar.

David set up camp in Germany, leasing an apartment in Berlin, a city still in the former East Germany and divided by the Berlin War. He began work on his twelfth album, *Low* (RCA) with Brian Eno. It was released in January 1977. It formed what Bowie dubbed the "Berlin triptych" along with *"Heroes"* and *Lodger*.

In February Bowie played keyboards in the band backing Iggy Pop on his US tour in March. The group included Hunt Sales (drums) and Tony Sales (bass) who helped Bowie form Tin Machine a decade later. Iggy, Bowie and the group went to the States for a 15-date tour in March and April before returning to Berlin.

1977 was a strange year for Bowie, fraught with gloom and tragedy, even though he had returned to Europe in search of inner peace and fulfilment. As part of his eagerness to experiment and try new musical settings he had sung duets

Left: David Bowie with longtime friend Mick Jagger on set for the video to accompany their Live Aid duet 'Dancing In The Street' in 1985.

Above left and right: David Bowie's stage presence was more sedate, post-Ziggy. (Left) *Station To Station*, 1976, (right) Serious Moonlight (1983).

before, notably with John Lennon on 'Fame'. So it seemed only right that he should sing-along with Marc Bolan, when guesting on his old friend's Granada TV show *Marc* in Manchester on September 9, 1977. Bolan had been making a comeback as a TV celebrity and host after the T.Rex string of hits had ended. The sixth and final show in the series would feature punk rockers Generation X and David Bowie.

A horde of music press reporters descended on the studio and they witnessed a chaotic sequence of events including backstage rows and technical problems. Bolan was delighted that Bowie had agreed to appear on the show and planned to sing a couple of numbers with him. After David sang his latest number ''Heroes'' the pair climbed onto a small stage clutching guitars and ready to rock on an improvised ditty called 'Standing Next To You'. A smiling Bowie could see Marc was highly excited about this historic moment, but just as they began to sing Bowie got an electric shock from the microphone and Bolan tripped over a mike stand and fell off the podium.

As a result of all the delays the studio electricians refused to do any overtime and "pulled the plugs" at 7pm, just as Bolan and Bowie were finally getting it together. Enough of their performance was salvaged on video to be transmitted later. Bowie returned to London by train after the show and then flew back to Berlin. Just a week later on September 16, 1977 Marc Bolan, the star of T.Rex who had helped define Glam Rock, died in a car crash. He had been returning home from night at the Speakeasy Club and Morton's Restaurant, in a purple Mini driven by his partner Gloria Jones. At 5am the car crashed into a tree on a bend in the road on the edge of Barnes Common. Gloria was badly injured and Marc was dead. Just four days later his funeral was held at Golders Green Crematorium on September 20.

David was devastated at the news. He and Marc had been recording demos together and had talked about future collaborations. David flew back from Switzerland to attend the funeral and set up a trust fund for Bolan's son Rolan.

Left: David Bowie performing with friend Marc Bolan on the television show *Marc* in 1977. Just a few weeks later, Bolan was killed in a car crash.

Above and Overleaf: Bowie on stage as part of 1976's *Station To Station* tour. He moved to Switzerland that year. Photograph by John Rowlands.

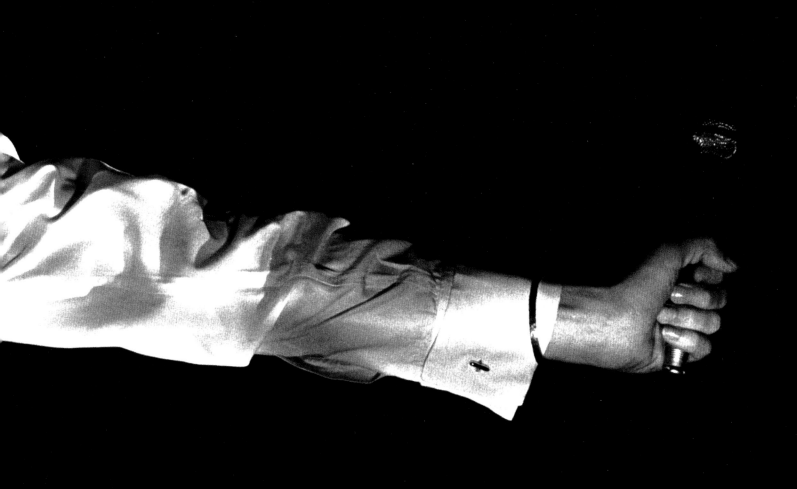

He experienced deep sorrow, as he went into mourning for his old friend.

Strangely, Bowie had undertaken another joint venture around this time, when he was invited to sing a duet with Bing Crosby, an artist who couldn't have been further from his normal musical associates such as Iggy Pop and Eno.

Crosby, the revered American crooner and movie star, was performing at the London Palladium during a UK tour that marked his return from semi-retirement. The star of *High Society* and the much loved Road movies with Bob Hope, was one of the world's biggest-selling recording artists and his 'White Christmas' remains a perennial favourite.

While celebrating Bing's 50th anniversary in show business it was proposed that Crosby and Bowie team up to sing 'The Little Drummer Boy' during filming for his *Merrie Olde Christmas* TV show in a London studio on September 11.

They appeared clad in identical blazers and Bing complimented his young partner on his singing and even asked for his home phone number. But they would never meet again.

Crosby died aged 74 from a heart attack while playing golf in Spain, just a month later, on October 14, 1977. Their joint TV appearance was shown later but the song wasn't a hit for another five years, when 'Peace On Earth, Little Drummer Boy' got to Number 3 in the UK charts in December 1982.

In 1981 Bowie teamed up with Freddie Mercury and Queen for their tensely dynamic 'Under Pressure'. The song's evolution began when David visited the Mountain Studio in Switzerland where Queen was working on a song by the band's drummer Roger Taylor called 'Feel It'. Bowie had originally been invited to sing backing vocals on another song called 'Cool Cat'. Later the band began jamming over simple piano fills, finger pops, handclaps and a suspense filled bass guitar line

Above: Bowie, as alien Thomas Jerome Newton, absorbs vital information from multiple screens in *The Man Who Fell To Earth*.

Right: Bowie again in front of a camera, as a Prussian officer on the set of *Just A Gigolo*, directed by David Hemmings and released in 1978.

devised by John Deacon. Bowie and Freddie Mercury began singing and 'Under Pressure' was born. Released as a single it shot to Number One in the U.K. chart in November 1981 and was featured on Queen's *Hot Space* (1981) album.

There was another musically appropriate liaison when he teamed up with fellow rock god Mick Jagger for a rousing version of 'Dancing In The Street' the old Martha & The Vandellas hit. Bowie and Jagger made a fun video of their dynamic performance which was show repeatedly on TV and at the historic Live Aid Concert at Wembley Stadium in July 1985. The single was a huge Number One hit and all the profits went to Live Aid.

Bowie would help celebrate the life and times of a fellow rock hero when he performed at the Freddie Mercury Tribute Concert For Aids Awareness held at London's Wembley Stadium on April 20, 1992. Freddie, the lead singer and song writing genius with Queen had died on November 24, 1991. The remaining members of Queen – Brian May, Roger Taylor and John Deacon – together

with their manager Jim Beach planned the memorial concert that would feature a galaxy of artists and groups who had admired or been influenced by Freddie and Queen's music.

Tickets for the show sold out in three hours and 72,000 packed the Stadium to see Metallica, Extreme, Def Leppard and Guns N'Roses perform their own sets. In the second half of the show Queen played with guests including Elton John, Roger Daltrey, Robert Plant, David Bowie, Mick Ronson, George Michael and Annie Lennox.

Bowie appeared in a lime green suit with neatly combed short hair, looking relaxed and confident as he sang 'Under Pressure' with Annie Lennox and Queen. Then Bowie, Ian Hunter, Mick Ronson, Joe Elliott and Phil Collen performed 'All The Young Dudes'. Bowie and his old Ziggy era mate Ronson together with Queen played "Heroes", a moving moment as Mick was already ill and this would be their last performance together. (Mick Ronson died from liver cancer aged 46 on April 29, 1993.)

David then surprised the vast audience – that included one billion TV viewers around the world – by falling to his knees and reciting The Lord's Prayer in support of another friend who was also terminally ill. It seemed like a dramatic, theatrical gesture, but it was heartfelt and sincere. Bowie still had the power to shock and capture moments in time.

Left: Bowie in *The Man Who Fell To Earth*, playing an alien sent to Earth to bring water back to his home planet. The film was directed by Nicolas Roeg.

Above: David Bowie chats with Queen's singer Freddie Mercury at London's Live Aid concert where they were both performing in 1985.

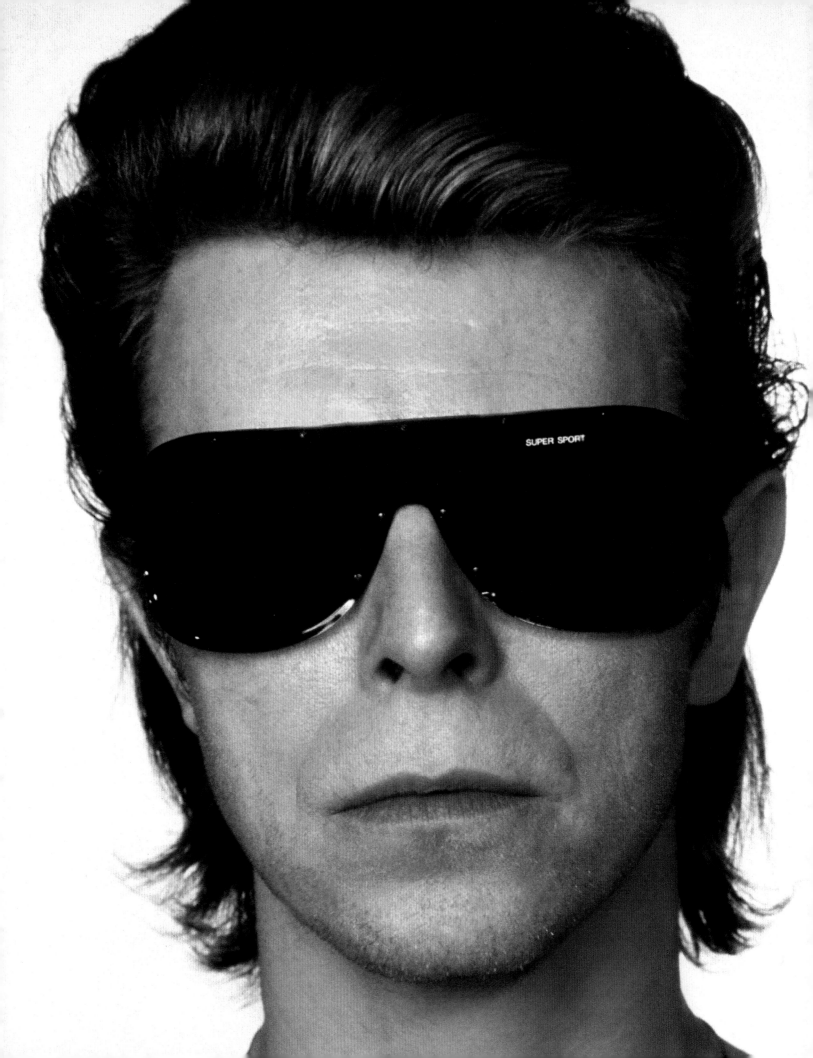

CHANGES

David Bowie was stricken by the tragic death of Marc Bolan in 1977, but there was even greater shock at the senseless murder of John Lennon in 1980. It was only five years earlier that Lennon and Bowie had formed the friendship that resulted in 'Fame' and whose advice had helped David find his way through the music business jungle.

It was while Bowie was performing in *The Elephant Man* at the Booth Theatre in New York that he heard the news that Lennon had been shot dead. On the night of December 8, 1980 John and Yoko Ono had been returning home to their apartment from a recording studio. As they were about to enter the Dakota Building John was shot five times by his assailant, Mark Chapman. Lennon died from loss of blood shortly afterwards at the Roosevelt hospital. Fans around the world were stunned. It was later discovered that Chapman had been to see a performance of *The Elephant Man* at the theatre just a few blocks away. A programme for the show was found in Chapman's hotel room with Bowie's name marked in black ink.

It was a frightening thought for many rock stars that they might now be in danger. Bowie abruptly ended his season in New York in early January 1981 and moved to Switzerland. After most of the year spent in quiet reflection and isolation, he ventured out to meet Queen who had arrived in Switzerland for recording sessions. It was then that he teamed up with Freddie and Queen to record 'Under Pressure'. The upbeat U.K. Number One was also a Top 30 hit in the States and marked the return of Bowie to mainstream pop after his "Berlin Triptych" of the late Seventies.

This was a musically challenging period that had begun with *Low* (1977), an album produced by Tony Visconti that underscored Bowie's break with 'rock' and a determined attempt to return to experimentation. Even while bands like Led Zeppelin and The Who were still enjoying enormous success Bowie pronounced "rock is dead" and was eager to draw a line under his own recent past.

Low also signalled David's departure from America and return to Europe where he began to work with like-minded souls, notably Brian Eno from Roxy Music and Robert Fripp, guitarist and founder of King Crimson. Bowie was fully aware of the possibilities presented by high tech recording, different instruments, computers and synthesizers. However the opening tracks on *Low* clearly retained crucial elements of rock with its pulsating beats, guitar riffs and souped up heavy drums.

Low was recorded at the Château d'Herouville, near Paris where David had recorded *Pin Ups* back in 1973 and produced Iggy Pop's album *The Idiot*. Originally the album was going to be called *New Music, Night And Day* and among contributors were

Carlos Alomar (guitars), Rickey Gardner (guitars), Dennis Davis (percussion), George Murray (bass), Roy Young (piano) and Brian Eno (keyboards). Bowie played a variety of instruments including keyboards, vibraphone and a xylophone.

The completed album, renamed *Low*, was released after some delay in January 1977 in an orange cover with a still picture of Bowie on the sleeve, taken from *The Man Who Fell To Earth*. The title reflected Bowie's mood after undergoing stressful business meetings and court case hearings in Paris, relating to his management dispute. There was also a bout of ill health to contend with caused by an outbreak of dysentery at the studio. The final mixing sessions were hastily relocated to Berlin's Hansa studio.

The first part of the album is devoted to relatively mainstream rock, utilizing extremely powerful drumming. Visconti had enhanced the snare drum sound in by using an Eventide Harmonizer, a technique that proved influential on many other producers and musicians.

The more experimental material was confined to the second half. Even so, the opening 'Speed Of Life' proved a surprise to RCA executives when they first heard the tapes as it entirely lacked any vocals. It's crashing beat certainly sets a mood of aggression further developed on 'Breaking Glass' where Bowie finally bursts into song with the memorable line "Baby I've been breaking glass in your room again".

'What In The World' kicks off with Dennis Davis' drums kicking with brute strength as David launches into a shouty blues club style rocker emphasizing the hook line "For Your Love" that might have been a bow to The Yardbirds' hit. 'Sound And Vision' has a Bo Diddley style rhythm, and features a minimalist set of lyrics. Nevertheless, this simplest of *Low* tracks got to Number 3 in the UK charts in March 1977.

'Always Crashing In The Same Car' has Ricky Gardner on lead guitar and Bowie muses on a well-intended life spent always looking backwards and forwards and undergoing intermittent crises. 'Be My Wife' has Bowie taking a more positive vocal role than on some of *Low*'s oddly disjointed performances as he sings in helpless fashion: "Sometimes you get so lonely, I've lived all over the world, please be mine…"

'A New Career In A New Town' is a reprise of the opening track in the sense there are no vocals at all by the mainman,

but it grooves along with harmonica taking the most of the instrumental space. One of *Low*'s most intriguing tracks is the carefully crafted 'Warszawa', a tonal piece devised by Brian Eno and Bowie and partly inspired by David's trip to the Polish capital Warsaw in 1976. He hoped to capture the bleak atmosphere of a city where the horrors of the Warsaw Ghetto under Nazi rule during the Second World War remained a grim memory. He achieves this by creating a slow, haunting piece of music with an underlying religious sentiment.

'Art Decade' is another tone poem with cello added by a studio engineer while 'Weeping Wall' is an instrumental full of strange melodic and percussion effects about the oppressive Berlin Wall, that was finally torn down in 1989. Such Bowie-Eno concepts impressed the American minimalist composer Philip Glass. He later composed the *Low Symphony* (1992) and *"Heroes"* (1996) another symphony based on these ground breaking Bowie albums.

The final track 'Subterraneans' is a piece David originally hoped to be used in the soundtrack for *The Man Who Fell To Earth* and is another mournful mainly instrumental piece over a doom-laden bass line, suggesting isolation and loss of identity, inspired by young people trapped in East Berlin. The mood is further emphasized by a mournful Bowie's saxophone and some desultory vocals. Despite lack of promotion and less than enthusiastic

reviews *Low* became a Gold album and got to Number 2 in the UK and Number 11 in the U.S. charts

The second album in the "Berlin Triptych", *"Heroes"* (RCA) was released on October 14, 1977 and the title song became one of Bowie's most triumphal hits. It was recorded at Hansa Studio in Berlin and the ten tracks were produced by Tony Visconti. Once again the commercial songs were slotted up front. David played keyboards, guitar, saxophone and koto and was joined by Carlos Alomar (rhythm guitar), Dennis Davis (percussion), George Murray (bass) and Robert Fripp (lead guitar).

Bowie conceded that *"Heroes"* wasn't a particularly happy album but the writing was done quickly and the recording took just two weeks. Much of the music was even deeper and harder to absorb than had appeared on *Low* and the influence of Germany's Kraftwerk was detectable on such items as 'V-2 Schneider'. The album is presented in a minimalist sleeve design with a striking black and white photograph of the artist by Sukita. The music was greeted with praise by those prepared to understand his determination to try something different. One fan called it: "An astounding piece of work, an act of courage".

It opens with 'Beauty And The Beast' on which Bowie chants "You can't say no to the beauty and the beast" in a piece that marches along with military precision, filled with menace and aggression. Released as a single in January 1978 it only managed to get to No.39 in the UK charts. 'Joe The Lion' is a cabaret-style vocal performance that pores over a drink or two in Joe's Beer House, a Berlin hostelry he frequented in search of company. Berlin bars, he said, were "for sad, disillusioned people to get drunk in". The piece was also perceived as a tribute to American performance artist Chris Burden.

Previous pages: Circa 1980. Ziggy was long gone, the Thin White Duke retired, and Bowie had moved on in terms of music and fashion.

Above left: Bowie with ex-Beatle John Lennon in New York in 1975.
Above right: David Bowie in Amsterdam, 1977.

Left: A serious-looking David Bowie on the set of *The Hunger*. The band Bauhaus make a brief appearance in the 1983 movie.

Above: A portrait of David Bowie from 1978. The striking difference in the two eyes – caused by a childhood accident – is clearly visible.

Overleaf: A massive fan following greets David Bowie on his 1996 Serious Moonlight concert tour: his largest and most successful ever.

Above: Portrait of David Bowie by prominent fashion photographer Norman Parkinson (1913–1990), London, circa 1977.

Right: Although the glam of Ziggy had gone, Bowie continued to be a hugely entertaining performer – art and music were always mixed.

"Heroes" was inspired by seeing two young people having an affair in the shadow of the Berlin Wall near a gun turret. He saw them as brave souls risking to profess their love in a dangerous situation and sings tragically on their behalf. "I will be king and you, you will be queen … we can be heroes just for one day".

When released as a single it heroically struggled to reached Number 24 in the UK chart but grew in stature and importance, notably when David sang it at Live Aid in 1985. 'Sons Of The Silent Age' is a riveting commentary or wake up call to those lifeless commuters with "blank looks and no books" travelling on their endless and purposeless journeys. David sings with operatic passion as he tries to attract the world's attention. 'Blackout' verges on hysteria as David recalls a collapse when he was rushed to a hospital in Berlin, suffering from a panic attack brought on by a visit by his wife. "Get me to a doctor's…get me some protection!" he pleads.

'V-2 Schneider' is a dramatic, doomy piece influenced by Kraftwerk's Florian Schneider whose group based in Düsseldorf specialised in experimental electronic sounds. They'd hit the US and UK charts with 'Autobahn' and Bowie and Florian had become friends. 'Sense Of Doubt' is a brave piece of writing that utilizes synthesizer and gloomy piano to suggest the mood of claustrophobia and fear induced by living in the walled city of Berlin. The same air permeates 'Moss Garden' a slow instrumental piece on which Bowie plays a Koto an unusual Japanese string instrument. The Japanese

moss garden is designed to induce feelings of calm and encourage meditation.

'Neuköln' is another descriptive musical portrait, this time of the Turkish quarter of Berlin, a community that led Bowie to experiment with his art in a series of paintings. His saxophone playing creates a mood of hopeless isolation. The final track 'The Secret Life Of Arabia' sees a return to a rhythmic pulse while Bowie sings of walking through the desert.

After the release of *"Heroes"*, Bowie began filming *Just A Gigolo* with Marlene Dietrich and director David Hemmings during December. Berlin remained his base, having left the home in Switzerland and he also embarked on holidays to Kenya and Japan. He travelled the globe, no longer afraid of flying.

On March 29, 1978 Bowie began a world tour that opened in San Diego and subsequently visited 65 cities. The North American part of the tour ended with three nights at Madison Square Garden in New York on May 7, 8 and 9. The European and British leg of the tour continued during May and June.

At the end of the UK tour in June Bowie began work with Eno on the next studio album *Lodger*. On September 25, 1978 RCA released Bowie's fifteenth album, the double LP *Stage* with 17 tracks spanning a range of material from Ziggy Stardust to 'Fame', 'Warszawa' and '"Heroes"'. It was all recorded live by Tony Visconti at concerts in Philadelphia, Providence and Boston during the US tour in April and May. The band had Carlos Alomar, Denis Davis and George Murray with Adrian Belew

Left: Portrait by Steve Schapiro, who has has shot classic photographs of David Bowie throughout his career.

Above left: David Bowie photographed by Christian Simonpietri in the workshop of Hungarian–French artist Victor Vasarely in 1977.

Above right: David Bowie and Annie Lennox performing at the Freddie Mercury Tribute Concert, April 29, 1992 at London's Wembley Stadium.

ex-Frank Zappa on lead guitar. The musicians were praised for reproducing the electronic sounds and special effects on the more demanding numbers from *Low* and *"Heroes"*.

In November the world tour resumed with seven concerts in Australia followed by three final shows in Osaka and Tokyo, Japan in December. David was back in London in February 1979 to attend the premiere of *Just A Gigolo* at the Prince Charles Cinema and to carry out promotional radio and TV interviews. On May 25 *Lodger* (RCA) was released featuring six tracks co-written with Brian Eno. David spent the rest of the year travelling between England, Switzerland and America and holidaying in Kenya, with little other musical activity beyond performing 'Space Oddity' on DJ Kenny Everett's New Year's Eve TV show.

Lodger was presented in gatefold sleeve with a peculiar Polaroid photograph of the artist sprawled out with his nose bent out of shape apparently as the result of an accident. The original album title was going to be *Planned Accidents*. The cover design also includes a symbolic postcard addressed to "David Bowie at RCA Records", hinting that the songs were like postcards from around the world.

It was the last of the so-called "Berlin Triptych" albums, but was actually recorded at Mountain Studios, Switzerland and at the Record Plant, New York in between legs of the 1978 world tour. Adrian Belew was featured on guitar, replacing Robert Fripp who had worked on *"Heroes"* and he was called upon to contribute experimental methods of playing, utilizing various takes performed to random backing tracks. The musicians were also asked to play different unfamiliar instruments, all part of the Bowie-Eno attempt to create new sounds and explore different possibilities.

Lodger differs from the previous two albums in that Bowie abandoned the policy of having one LP side of vocal numbers and one of instrumentals. Instead it had two major themes, one about world travel and the other a critique of Western civilization.

There were no obvious hit tracks although 'Boys Keep Swinging' was released with 'Fantastic Voyage' on the B-side as a single in April 1979. *Lodger* received less attention than was usual for a Bowie album, although it is now conceded to be underrated. At the end of the Seventies the now older and more mature artist was being upstaged by punk rockers, New Romantics and heirs to Bowie's own tradition, such as electro pop singer Gary Numan, who regarded Bowie as the Godfather rather than a fellow young rebel.

Even loyal Bowie fans were beginning to have their patience stretched with the insistence of their hero in being quite so consistently gloomy and introspective. It may have been an attempt to rectify the situation that Bowie then made three lively promo videos for the album featuring 'Boys Keep Swinging', 'DJ' and

Above: David Bowie on stage at London's Wembley Stadium in July 1995 at the Live Aid concert for famine relief.

Right: David Bowie, smart as ever in crisp suit and with dyed hair, in concert as part of the Serious Moonlight tour of 1983.

'Look Back In Anger' with director David Mallet from the *Kenny Everett Video Show*.

David dressed up in drag for 'Boys Keep Swinging' and also played each of his three 'female' backing singers. For these roles he wore a variety of outfits and wigs including a polka dot dress, gold lame gown and a woolly cardigan.

He performed the number on Everett's TV show in April and the record got to Number 7 in the UK in June. It was a surprise move to return to his old gay, glittery androgynous image after spending two years specializing in deadly serious music. It marked the end of his Eno association as he bid goodbye to Berlin.

David was now living in a loft apartment in New York and ready to cope with life in America, having recovered health and spirits during his exile in Berlin. The title of the album was deemed to have been inspired either by the Roman Polanski film *The Tenant* or Alfred Hitchcock's 1926 silent movie classic *The Lodger*. The character himself was supposedly a homeless wanderer victimized by life's pressures.

Although not hugely popular, *Lodger* did get to Number 4 in the UK and Number 20 in the US and Bowie spent a good deal of effort promoting it around the world. The opening lightweight song 'Fantastic Voyage' has David emphasizing he doesn't want to "Live with somebody's depression" and talks of dignity and loyalty, reflecting no doubt on his own turbulent life and ever present threat of nuclear war. "It's a very modern world but nobody is perfect" he observes sagely.

'African Night Flight' abounds with jungle noises produced in combination with Eno who is credited with providing the "cricket menace" effect. The result of safari holidays in Kenya combined with a parody of W.H. Auden's poem *Night Mail*, the track becomes an unnerving African cocktail of chants and drones. 'Move On' has David the traveller packing his bag, taking a train or sailing at dawn and confirming "I'm just a travelling man" as he voyages from Africa to Russia and Cyprus. Part of the arrangement was the result of Bowie playing old tape recordings backwards and adding vocal harmonies with Tony Visconti. 'Move On' excited Bowie. It celebrated a return to an "up" mood after the "down" of his previous two albums.

'Yassassin' is an inspired excursion into world music whose title means "long live" in Turkish. Simon House adds suitably Eastern style violin as Bowie informs the world against a Jamaican reggae beat, "I'm not a moody guy … just a working man, no judge of

Left: On June 28, 1977, punk rock was at the height of fashion in the UK. David Bowie, having paved the way in fashion, had already moved on…

men". It works. 'Red Sails' presents an unfocussed blend of ideas and images including the concept of a swashbuckling English mercenary sailing in the China Sea. Bowie called it a "cross-reference of cultures".

'DJ' is much more successful as a rocking collaboration between Bowie, Eno and Alomar. Bowie's opening salvo includes the attention commanding line "I'm home, lost my job and incurably ill. You think this is easy". It's a paean to those DJs who had become all powerful in a music business increasingly dominated by the tastes and demands of disco and club goers. 'DJ' was released as a single but failed to get higher than 29 in the UK chart.

'Look Back In Anger' was originally going to be the album's title and is a fast-paced rocker that sounds not unlike Led Zeppelin on tracks such as 'Immigrant Song' or 'Achilles Last Stand'. The lyrical theme is about angels of death and the title comes from John Osborne's 1956 play.

'Boys Keeping Swinging' stomps along with glee as it returns to pop music in a simpler age. In an attempt to recreate musical innocence Carlos Alomar plays drums and Dennis Davis switches to bass, playing like a garage band discovering rock 'n' roll. 'Repetition' concerns itself with the subject of wife beating, based on stories Bowie had read in U.S. newspapers. One concerns a man hitting his wife because she provides cold dinners when he comes home from work. "What's the use of me working when you can't damn cook?" is the grim message delivered in deadpan style over a dirge like beat.

Final track 'Red Money' has more synthesizer from Roger Powell who joined the team in the studio at Eno's behest. Bowie described the song as being about responsibility and having to learn to deal with high finance.

The new decade began with Bowie on working on *Scary Monsters (And Super Creeps)* (RCA) at the Power Station in New York. February 1980 was also the month when his divorce from Angela became final and Bowie took custody of their son Duncan. With the aim of keeping a higher musical profile, Bowie released the single 'Alabama Song' coupled with an acoustic version of 'Space Oddity' that month. He also continued his travels, going to Japan to make TV commercials and on to Berlin to play keyboards with Iggy Pop on stage.

Previous pages, left: David Bowie caught in a moment of amusement in 1983, the year of the Serious Moonlight global tour.

Previous pages, right: David Bowie in 1978. Seen here performing on stage at the Sports Arena in San Diego, California, USA.

Above: Bowie on stage at Newcastle City Hall in June 1978 as part of the *Low/"Heroes"* world tour which began in March of that year.

Right: David in Paris to perform at the Pavillon in 1976. It was an industrial-looking venue that suited Bowie's music of that period.

résente
DAVID
17, 18, 19 MAI/20 H.
PAVILLON DE PARIS
PORTE DE PANTIN.
LOCATION: PAV. PARIS
OLYMPIA/3 FNAC.

In May he completed *Scary Monsters* and come July made his acting debut in *The Elephant Man* in Denver. The new album was released on September 12 and would be his last for RCA. The year was darkened by the death of John Lennon in December and after completing his acting commitments in New York Bowie returned his home in Switzerland to live in seclusion.

Scary Monsters is an angry and powerful work, with Bowie setting his monsters free. The mood is established from the start with 'It's No Game (Part 1)' where Bowie sounds like Lennon in his primeval screaming mode letting it all hang out, while the paranoid lyrics are also delivered by a macho girl in Japanese, making it sounds all the more violent and intense.

'Up The Hill Backwards' has acoustic guitars played by producer Visconti and is about people trying to lead normal lives while bombarded with images of catastrophes. The fast-moving neurotic 'Scary Monsters' deals with a relationship and a "scary" girl with blues eyes and a dangerous mind who could easily have been a killer. Bowie drifts briefly into his best South London gangster accent that must have sounded scary to New Yorkers.

'Ashes To Ashes' is the most attractive song from the album and became his biggest hit in some years when it finally got to Number One in the UK charts in August 1980. It sat well with the New Romantic and Techno Pop movement of the early Eighties when bands like Human League were making an impact.

Amusingly Bowie reintroduces the main character from 'Space Oddity' into the lyrics saying "We know Major Tom's a junkie". The promo video directed by David Mallet gave Bowie a surreal image, in which dressed as a clown with a white face and pointed hat he is chased by a bulldozer on the shores of a black sea bathed in red light.

'Fashion' is a grinding poke at disco dance crazes and the threat of cultural fascism. It contains both a mind bending guitar solo and the quaint announcement from Bowie that: "We are the Goon Squad and we're coming to town". Along with 'Scary Monsters', here was a more pop-conscious Bowie, still retaining his commendable desire to experiment with cutting-edge ideas. 'Fashion' accompanied by a hot video set in a dance studio and on New York streets was another hit and got to Number 5 in the UK.

Above: Bowie in Berlin. Portrait of the man on his bed by Denis O'Regan in 1983, although Bowie's classic "Berlin" era was 1976–1979.

Right: David Bowie at the foot of the Berlin Wall in 1987. The city has always played an important part in Bowie's life, and vice versa.

'Teenage Wildlife' has David musing "How come you only want tomorrow with its promise of something hard to do". It's a rather agonized look at his own position as a former teenage pop star still expected to cut capers. 'Scream Like A Baby' is a surreal blend of influences that is more disturbing than enjoyable while 'Kingdom Come' is a cover of a song by Tom Verlaine of American group Television.

'Because You're Young', the penultimate item, is a rather forgettable theme but lifts the general mood amidst the long march back to pop and rock. *Scary Monsters* closes with a reprise of 'It's No Game (Part 2)' sung in English rather than Japanese. It contains the chilling line "Put a bullet in my brain and it makes all the papers – it's no game".

In the two years after John Lennon's death Bowie spent much of the time in Switzerland keeping a low media profile but still engaging in acting roles and making music notably 1981's happy collaboration with Queen, 'Under Pressure'. However there was real pressure when his half-brother Terry Burns attempted suicide in June 1982 and David rushed to visit him in hospital. Burns

attempted suicide again in December 1984 by lying across a railway track in South London and was injured. He made another attempt two weeks later at the same spot and this time was killed by an express train. Distressed, Bowie sent flowers to the funeral from his home in Switzerland.

1982 was spent filming *The Hunger* and *Merry Christmas Mr. Lawrence* and David also appeared in a BBC TV production of Bertholt Brecht's play *Baal*. By January 1983 Bowie had left RCA and signed a new deal with EMI America that ensured he had to deliver three albums over the next five years.

His first release for EMI America was *Let's Dance*, that resulted in a UK and US Number 1 hit single with the title track in April. The album was produced by Nile Rodgers and featured guest guitar player Stevie Ray Vaughan. It was the biggest selling album of his career thus far. Among the highlights are such pop songs as 'Modern Love' that reveal Bowie's new "trust in God". Released as a single it reached Number 2 in the UK.

'China Girl', a Bowie/Iggy Pop collaboration accompanied by a sensuous promo video, provided yet another hit.

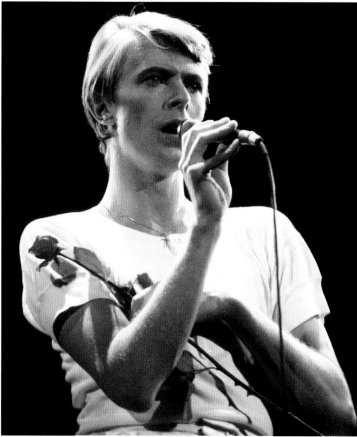

It shot to Number 10 in the US and Number 2 in the UK, even though the promo video was banned by BBC TV for being "too sexy". The echoing 'Let's Dance' is a cleverly simple production and among the remaining tracks, Stevie Ray Vaughan's guitar stands out on 'Cat People (Putting Out The Fire)', while 'Shake It' is a real dance floor groover.

In May that year Bowie went off on the Serious Moonlight 83 World Tour in Belgium followed by British dates with three nights at Wembley Arena in June. The tour continued across America in July with Bowie travelling in his own Boeing 707 before visiting New Zealand, Australia and Japan.

The tour ended in Thailand in December, 1983. Bowie returned with a new studio album *Tonight* (EMI America) in September 1984 that yielded two hit singles: 'Loving The Alien' that got to Number 19 in the UK in June, and 'Blue Jean' Number 6 in September. Recorded in Canada, the album was generally regarded as a disappointment by Bowie fans even though 'Absolute Beginners' – used as the title song from the movie – got to Number 2 in the UK in March 1986.

In April 1987 came Bowie's twentieth album *Never Let Me Down* (EMI) recorded at Mountain Studios, Switzerland with Carlos Alomar and Peter Frampton on guitars. Among the more popular tracks 'Day-In Day-Out' got to number 17 in the UK. One of the more experimental tracks, 'Glass Spider', has a narrative more

Spinal Tap than Ziggy Stardust.

The Glass Spider World Tour that accompanied the album was a massive stage production featuring a 60-foot high fibreglass spider. Bowie himself appeared out of the jaws of the neon-lit monster wearing a red suit while scampering energetically around the stage in what was an expensive and eye-boggling production. During the six month tour he was accompanied by Peter Frampton on guitar and half a dozen musicians and dancers. David himself described the tour as "enormously strenuous". Perhaps it was with a sense of relief that on the last night of the tour, the Glass Spider was symbolically set on fire.

A year later David formed Tin Machine, his first group since the Spiders From Mars. Deemed as a reaction against the excesses of the Glass Spider Tour, he set aside his own fame to team up as an equal in a joint venture with guitarist Reeves Gabrels, drummer Hunt Sales and bassist Tony Sales. They recorded *Tin Machine* in Switzerland in April 1988. Released in May 1989, it got to Number 3 in the UK and 28 in the US despite some discouraging reviews.

The group's concert debut was in New York on June 14, with Bowie insisting he was just a sideman in the group and not the star. From Glass Spider to Tin Machine, Bowie had made yet another dramatic move and he still had the 1990s and more mountains to climb and achievements to celebrate.

Opposite, left: David Bowie with striking blond hair and three-piece suit, at a meeting in Tokyo in 1983. He played four nights at the Budokan.

Opposite, right: David Bowie performing, circa 1977. He later penned 'Pretty Pink Rose' for Adrian Belew on *Young Lions* (1990).

Above: David on stage in Chicago, Ill, USA, in August 1983, in full swing on the Serious Moonlight tour of that year.

STILL A
STARMAN

Tin Machine was a bold move by Bowie, now happy to take a more democratic role as just another guy in the band. His new group certainly had serious musical aspirations, as might be expected given the abilities and strong personalities within in the project. Hunt and Tony Sales had both worked with Bowie on Iggy Pop's *Lust For Life* album and Reeves Gabrels was Bowie's new guitar partner, replacing Carlos Alomar.

Bowie had met Gabrels during the 1987 Glass Spider tour at a time when he said he had lost his vision and wanted to get back into creating live music, devoid of machines and effects. Gabrels offered enthusiastic advice and Bowie found him a lifeline to get him back on track. He then approached Tony Sales at an end of tour party to help form the band together with Hunt.

The brash and exuberant heavy rock sound of *Tin Machine* (EMI) may have come as a shock to those whose expectations were based on Bowie's past output but it was clearly superior to anything he'd done on albums such as *Never Let Me Down*. The roaring power of tracks like 'Heaven's In Here' offered welcome relief after Glass Spider, for example. The tracks were recorded 'live' with no overdubs and the songs had a hard edge, with angry themes like 'Crack City', a song about the drugs and urban decay observed by these hardened musicians as they travelled the world.

Tin Machine made its European tour debut at La Cigale, Paris in June 1989 before heading to England for a brace of concerts. They drew crowds of loyal supporters who David revealed with pride called themselves "The Tinnies".

Several weeks were spent in Australia rehearsing and recording during July before releasing the single 'Tin Machine' coupled with 'Maggie's Farm' in August. In October came another single 'Prisoner Of Love' with a live version of 'Baby Can't Dance' on the B-side. The band then moved from Australia to New York for further recording sessions.

While Tin Machine was struggling to establish its identity and convince the record company of their viability, the identity of Bowie the Megastar could not be forgotten. He had been making headlines, music and hit records for some 25 years by the start of the Nineties and it was time to celebrate his achievements.

In January 1990 a retrospective collection of his work called *Sound + Vision* (Rykodisc) comprising all of his previous 18 albums was released on different formats including vinyl, CD and cassette tape, repackaged with extra tracks. A special wooden boxed CD set even came with letters of certification signed by Bowie. Although it was a North American release by the Canadian label Rykodisc, copies were imported into the UK. David promoted

Previous page: A 1996 portrait of David Bowie by Kevin Cummins.
Above: Ever the showman, David Bowie dresses up for every performance, circa 2000.

Opposite: A 1993 portrait of David Bowie by Albert Sanchez for *Movieline's Hollywood Life* magazine.

the collection by announcing a six-month world tour that would visit 15 countries and feature over 100 concerts where he'd play his greatest hits "for the last time". It was an epic journey that would earn Bowie some £20 million and the *Sound + Vision* compilation would win a Grammy Award for its packaging.

The tour began in Quebec, Canada on March 4, 1990 and in August Bowie performed two shows in England at Milton Keynes Bowl. That same month tragedy ensued when the guitarist and singer/songwriter Stevie Ray Vaughan, who had played on Bowie's *Let's Dance* album, died in a helicopter crash after performing with Double Trouble at an Eric Clapton concert in Wisconsin. Vaughan, the pilot and all the other passengers were killed when the helicopter flew into a hill in fog on August 27, 1990.

In September Bowie played to an audience of 100,000 fans in Buenos Aires, Argentina – the first British artist to play there since the Falklands War in 1982. Bowie's next group album *Tin Machine II* was launched with a party in Los Angeles in August 1991 attended by Little Richard, Bowie's rock 'n' roll idol. The album was released in the UK by London Records on September 2, having been recorded in Australia at the end of 1989. Its release had been delayed by the *Sound + Vision* tour and an ongoing disagreement with the record company. As a result Bowie had left EMI and in March 1991 signed to Victory whose records were distributed by London. Among the best tracks on the new album were high-speed rocker 'Baby Universal' the poppy 'Goodbye Mr. Ed' and dramatic 'Shopping For Girls'. In October 1991 Tin Machine began a world tour in Europe playing small venues, with eight concerts in Britain, including two in Brixton in November. The final show took place in Tokyo February 17, 1992. The group's third album *Tin Machine Live: Oy Vey, Baby* (Victory) was released on July 27, 1992, its title a pun on U2's Eno-produced hit album *Achtung Baby*. It failed to even dent the charts – a rare event for a David Bowie record.

David was in Los Angeles in July 1992 when he talked about how important Tin Machine had been to him at a crucial turning point in his career. Asked about the reaction to the band during its six-month trek he replied cheerily: "It's been absolutely splendid. I think we have an audience now. How can you argue with a sell-out tour?"

But he acknowledged the press criticism of himself and the group: "I think a lot of people feel let down when a person like myself changes so radically. I know because I've had it thrown at me. There's also the memory thing, where people want to hold on to what they knew in the past. Everybody seems to have their favourite David Bowie period."

He felt there were too many preconceptions about what he and the band should be doing. "We would only start worrying about hostile press if it started to affect people coming to see us, which manifestly hasn't happened. This band has sold out in every place it's played in every country, need I say more? For us it has been a major success."

Yet the decision to form Tin Machine was almost foolhardy in some eyes. "Yes, I did the most absurd thing. Most lead singers of bands yearn to break free and become a solo artist. I did the very opposite. There was I, a very successful solo artist that decided that I didn't want that for the time being.

"I've got to be honest, I had some very desperate times thinking about what I was doing, realizing that it was a really abrupt, radical thing to do with my life, not singing any of my old stuff anymore and breaking ties with the past. But it was very important for me to do that. I felt marvellous about the decision. I just felt that at my age I was accomplishing something essential to me and my writing. I still feel the spark of excitement.

"Nor is it anything to do with 'doing a teenage thing'. It's about where to find the excitement and aggression for being alive at different ages of your life."

Bowie was now middle aged and still expected to rock like a teen idol. He didn't see that as a problem. "I'm 45 with 50 not far off and I'm still an emotional, excitable man. I find that in my loves, in my attitude to life and the things I like to buy as music. There is still a flame burning. This is a way of keeping that fire kindled. The most important thing with Tin Machine is we are able to play what we want without compromise. It's a very creative environment and the material is much more the kind of thing I was doing with *Scary Monsters (And Super Creeps)*. *Oy Vey Baby* will show people who haven't seen us, what this band is about live".

David promised a third studio album would be made in October 1992 and adding: "This band is going to be around for a long time yet". In fact Tin Machine's record sales were disappointing and the third studio album never happened. Thereafter the band dissolved and Bowie returned to his work as a solo artist.

On April 5, 1993 Bowie unveiled *Black Tie White Noise* (Arista) his first solo album since 1987's *Never Let Me Down*. Much of the impetus for his new burst of creativity was credited to happier circumstances in his personal life.

In October 1990 David had met Iman Abdulmajid, the internationally famous supermodel. She was born in Mogadishu, Somalia on July 25, 1955. Her forename name means "faith" in Arabic. The daughter of a diplomat and former ambassador to

Saudi Arabia, she moved to America where she began a modelling career for *Vogue* magazine.

Fluent in five languages, the beautiful Iman was also an actress and successful business woman. Formerly married to US baseball player Spencer Heywood, she divorced in 1987. After Bowie split with Melissa Hurley he and Iman became an item and romance blossomed. David proposed marriage while at dinner on a river boat floating down the Seine in Paris in October 1991. Iman accepted and the couple began house hunting.

Just a few days after Bowie performed his famed duet with Annie Lennox at the 1992 Freddie Mercury tribute concert in Wembley, David and Iman were married. The ceremony took place in Lausanne, Switzerland on April 24, 1992. On June 6 they held a church wedding at St. James Episcopal Church in Florence and among the celebrity guests were Yoko Ono, Bono from U2, Brian Eno, Jerry Hall, Bianca Jagger, David's 21-year-old son Duncan Jones and his 78-year-old mother Peggy. The beautiful couple left

shortly afterwards for a honeymoon in France. David had at last found the love of his life, sweeping away the unhappiness that had gripped him in the past.

The new album was produced by Nile Rodgers who had last worked with Bowie on *Let's Dance* in 1983. The tracks included an instrumental written for Iman, called 'The Wedding' that blended elements of Church of England and Muslim faiths in musical form. David told reporters: "It was played at the church but without the drums!" 'Pallas Athena' is another instrumental named after the god who leapt fully armed from the head of Jupiter. "I had to write the music for the service myself because

Above: David Bowie in New York City in 1997. He lived in the city most of the time after moving there in the early 1990s.

Right: David Bowie on stage at the Ritz Stockholm, Sweden, March 28, 1987, as part of the Glass Spider tour, which continued until the end of that year.

I didn't want either family to be uncomfortable. I couldn't use hymns, so I wrote this music which incorporated what I felt were our feelings towards one another. I was trying to capture both our worlds."

On the vocal tracks there was a welcome a return to form by Bowie, whose voice had begun to sound hoarse in recent years, no doubt as a result of competing with loud musicians on stage, as well as his long term nicotine habit.

Instead of emphasizing lead guitar, the new tracks featured the trumpet playing of Lester Bowie while David also played more saxophone. Outstanding among the 14 tracks is 'Jump They Say' about the life and death of Bowie's brother Terry who had been so influential towards David in guiding him towards jazz music and literature. Released as a single it became David's first Top Ten hit in seven years.

David paid tribute to Scott Engel of the Walker Brothers (a Bowie fan) with a cover of Scott's 'Nite Flights' and a version of Cream's hit 'I Feel Free' had Mick Ronson on guitar, making what turned out to be his last performance on a Bowie album. It was the first project their pair had worked on for 20 years. David: "We kept track of each other through the years. When I'd go on tour Mick would turn up somewhere and guest on my show.

"It was just synchronistic that we happened to be in the same city at the same time. I asked him if he'd work on a song we both liked very much which was Cream's 'I Feel Free'. He turned up and played a breathtaking solo. Extraordinary man and an extraordinary guitar player."

Another surprise on the album is a passionate vocal performance by Bowie on a cover of Morrissey's 'I Know It's Gonna Happen Someday'. Bowie: "It's just the silliest song I think Morrissey's written, but it's very cute." David had just heard an album by Morrissey and was under the impression he was 'spoofing' one of Bowie's earliest songs. "I thought, 'I'm not going to let him get away with that'. So took his song and did it my way. It got very incestuous because Mick Ronson produced Morrissey's album."

Bowie talked about his reunion with Nile Rodgers: "Some people thought it might be 'Son Of Let's Dance'. Silly people. They should know me better than that. So many things happen by coincidence. Nile came to the last Tin Machine shows in New York. We went to a club which is Nile's favourite place to hang out and talked about how we both liked dance music and hip hop. But I love a good strong melody line, so I said 'Let's try and do something together where we utilize a strong melody over that kind of music.' He was getting bored with the continual chant of dance music, so we decided to try and bring back a songwriting form to it."

The title track 'Black Tie White Noise' was written as a description of riots that has occurred in Los Angeles in 1992 as

a result of a white police beating of black citizen Rodney King. Bowie and Iman had witnessed the ensuing disturbances on the very day they'd flown back into LA. Recalled David: "Columns of thick black smoke were going into the sky and at night there were glows of fires everywhere. It was like a prison riot as if the inmates of some vast prison were trying to break out and free from their bonds. It was a war situation and very affecting."

Looking back over his past albums Bowie could see himself undergoing different moods and transitional periods, such as his need to take on the world with *Ziggy Stardust…* and the depression he felt between *Station To Station* and *Low*. "There's a great sadness in those albums. They did reflect those years when I was spiritually and emotionally sunk down. This one feels so positive and enthusiastic about everything. Writing really comes from the heart. And God is now central to my life although I don't have any persuasion towards an organized religion. I do have a strong knowledge that my life is not in my control, and that's something that's been reinforced over the last ten years. I had to believe I was in control of my own destiny. Now of course I know I was very wrong. It's easy to laugh at ideas, and it's much harder to believe."

Above: Bowie performing in Prague on the *Reality* tour, June 23, 2004.
Opposite: On stage at New York's legendary Madison Square Garden during the *Reality* tour, December 15, 2003.

Overleaf: A portrait of David Bowie by photographer Kate Garner, for the US-based *Ray Gun* magazine, March 1, 1996.

The album was released in the UK on Arista and on the small Savage label in the US. While *Black Tie White Noise* topped the UK charts it was hampered in the States by the abrupt financial collapse of Savage.

1994 began with Bowie recording with Brian Eno again for the first time in 15 years with sessions taking place in Switzerland attended by Reeves Gabrels, Mike Garson, Carlos Alomar, Erdal Kizilcay (bass) and Sterling Campbell (drums). Pop music had never been Bowie's total obsession and David the Renaissance Man had begun to concentrate on painting and the art world in general, buying paintings and putting on exhibitions. In February 1995 he went to Johannesburg with Iman for a *Vogue* photo shoot with Nelson Mandela. He completed a series of paintings and in April held his first solo art exhibition, New Afro/Pagan And Work 1975–1995, at London's Cork Street Gallery in Mayfair that featured his paintings, drawings and sculptures.

In September 1995, he embarked on his first world tour in five years. The Outside Tour supported the release on September 26 of his latest album *Outside* (Virgin) recorded with Eno. It began in Hartford, Connecticut on September 14 accompanied throughout the US dates by industrial rockers Nine Inch Nails a pairing that polarized fans. British dates began with three concerts at Wembley Arena on November 14, 15 and 17 with singer/songwriter Morrissey as Bowie's support act. Some sections of the audience began to leave shows half way through, as they found Bowie's new music "too difficult".

Outside was a concept album also known as *The Ritual Art-Murder Of Baby Grace Blue: A Non-Linear Gothic Drama Hyper-Cycle* and utilized images from ritual art and neo-paganism. It deals with the fictional murder of Baby Grace Blue, a 14-year-old victim of an underground craze for so-called art crime involving murder and mutilation, and the investigation into her death by one Professor Nathan Adler. Musically it blends a multitude of styles from avant garde jazz to techno revealed on such controversial tracks as the monotonous 'Hearts Filthy Lesson'. One of three albums tracks promoted as a single, its video full of images of death was deemed so disturbing that MTV refused to screen it in its original version.

Bowie and Eno's master plan had been to make a series of albums that would encapsulate the anxieties of the final five years of the 20th century, not realizing that the first five years of the 21st century would be even more stressful. It had intended to present a follow-up album called *Contamination* but in the event *Outside* was the only one compiled out of the many hours of recorded material available.

Bowie maintained his output however, releasing *Earthling* in February 1997 that was well received and got to Number 6 in the UK. David, who celebrated his 50th birthday on January 8, 1997 was now making a conscious attempt to reach out to younger audiences who weren't even born when he released his first hit albums. His next three albums *Hours…* (1999), *Heathen* (2002) and *Reality* (2003) were all Top Ten UK hits and were given glowing reviews.

Whenever Bowie appeared he was feted by those who had grown up regarding him as their ultimate pop idol, including the then Labour leader Tony Blair who had presented David with a Lifetime Achievement Award at the 1996 Brit Awards. He continued to be showered with awards and hailed by America's *Entertainment Weekly* as the Top Classic Solo Artist of all time, beating Elvis Presley and was inducted into the Rock And Roll Hall of Fame. He even became 'Dr. Bowie' when he was awarded an honorary music doctorate by California's Berklee College of Music and honoured by the French nation when he was made a Commander of Arts and Letters. David was voted Most Stylish Man Of the Year by *GQ* magazine in 2000 and consistently featured in music press awards. He could even have become 'Sir David Bowie' but politely declined the honour of a Knighthood.

An historic event took place on October 2, 2000 when Bowie returned to the Odeon Hammersmith, where he'd played thirty years earlier with the Spiders From Mars. A celebrity packed audience saw him play songs from *Heathen*, classic album tracks and climaxing with a heartfelt 'Ziggy Stardust' sung with a newly energised Bowie voice, thanks to his decision to finally quit smoking.

He hit the road once more for a massive tour to support *Reality*, in October 2003. The tour continued around the UK, US, Canada, New Zealand, Australia and Japan during 2004. It was very successful financially and musically, but exhausting for the star and fraught with incidents.

When Bowie was performing at a festival in Oslo, Norway on June 18 an excitable fan accidentally threw a lollipop towards the stage which hit him in the eye. The show had to be stopped while he recovered. Then on June 23 he became seriously ill while performing in Prague in the Czech Republic. He had to leave the stage once more.

He tried to carry on but was in agony from an unsuspected heart problem. A couple of days later after performing in Scheessel, Germany he felt worse and was taken to a hospital in Hamburg where he was found to have a blocked artery. He underwent an angioplasty to increase the flow of blood around his heart.

The rest of his European dates were cancelled and David flew home and spent time resting and recuperating. His heavy touring days over, although rumours persisted of one more farewell outing by the artist, now in his early Sixties. In June 2012 EMI reissued a special 40th anniversary edition of *Ziggy Stardust And The Spiders From Mars*. If fans around the world were still hungry for another glimpse into the world of David Bowie, all they had to do was listen and look at his vast legacy of sounds and visions.

"Look up, I'm in heaven."

David Bowie's shock death from cancer on Sunday, January 10, 2016 stunned his fans and unleashed a tidal wave of emotion that resonated around the world. When the announcement came the following Monday morning, the media responded with unprecedented coverage for a British rock star who had become an international icon.

His death came just days after the surprise release of his new album *Blackstar* on the day of his 69th birthday, January 8. It was already heading to the top, but it shot to Number One in the UK chart following the sad news.

The star had been ill for some 18 months, but his battle with pancreatic cancer had not been made public. However, it soon became clear that the lyric to his song 'Lazarus', selected from the album as a single, with its poignant line "Look up here, I'm in heaven" was a final, farewell message.

In the wake of his demise TV and radio stations made Bowie their main news story and the following day newspaper were packed with pages of stories and pictures. Out on the streets fans gathered to sing his songs and place floral tributes in demonstrations of genuine grief and sorrow from New York and London to St Petersburg and Berlin.

There was an air of celebration too when crowds gathered on the Monday evening in Brixton, the South London suburb where he was born. Images of Bowie were projected on buildings and some 2,000 people joined in an impromptu singalong, accompanied by guitar-strumming street musicians outside the famous Ritzy Cinema. The lyrics from 'Starman' echoed through the night air along with exultant cries of "Rebel Rebel" and an equally cosmic 'Space Oddity'.

It was the sort of spontaneity and expression of love that would have delighted the London boy.

Although it appeared as if David Bowie had retreated from the world during the previous ten years, following ominous first signs of heart problems in 2003, the truth is he still showed a tenacious capacity to surprise with new ideas and fresh and creative music.

His final Reality Tour, completed in 2004, was said to have grossed some £41 million, so he was well placed to take a deserved rest. During his career he had written 700 songs and sold 140 million albums worldwide, earning him a significant fortune to leave to his heirs. So there was no real need to keep on re-inventing himself in some quest for a new Ziggy, Aladdin Sane or Thin White Duke.

Yet David Bowie, singer, composer, artist, actor and philanthropist needed to exercise the right to self-expression and retain the option to take on at least some work. He was also well aware of the need to

please his fans and "the biz" with some signs of activity.

Meanwhile David spent his time enjoying a quiet life with his wife Iman and their daughter Alexandria at their New York City home. Although full-length tours were now out of the question after his 2004 heart issues, he did make a few one off intermittent appearances on stage and in the recording studio.

In 2004 he recorded a duet on his old hit 'Changes' with Butterfly Boucher for the animated film *Shrek 2*. He also provided vocals for the song '(She Can) Do That' for another film, *Stealth*. He even appeared on stage with Canadian band Arcade Fire at the TV event 'Fashion Rocks' in September 2005. And there was a reunion with old friend Lou Reed on the album *No Balance Palace* (2005) by Danish band Kashmir.

In 2006 Bowie was awarded a Grammy Lifetime Achievement Award, showing that despite his unofficial retirement, he hadn't been forgotten by a grateful music industry. Although he firmly announced, "I'm taking a year off, no touring and no albums" he made a guest appearance, singing with Pink Floyd's Dave Gilmour at the London's Royal Albert Hall in May that year for an event recorded for posterity.

He also sang in November 2006 with Alicia Keys at the Black Ball, a New York charity event. However, it was the last time he would perform his music on stage.

In January 2010 came a double 'live' album *Reality Tour*, featuring material from his 2003 concert tour. Then his long rumoured 'farewell' album was suddenly announced on January 8, 2013 on his 66th birthday. Entitled *The Next Day* it was released on March 8. It was his first studio album in ten years. Once again the icon had taken Bowie watchers by surprise.

On Bowie's website it was stated: "In recent years radio silence has been broken only endless speculation, rumour and wishful thinking. A new record, who would have ever thought it, who'd ever dreamed it!" Indeed.

The Next Day, produced by Bowie's old friend Tony Visconti was accompanied by the single 'Where Are We Now?' together with a visually captivating video directed by Tony Oursler. Visconti, acting as Bowie's spokesman, affirmed that the singer had no intention of going back on tour and just wanted to concentrate on making records.

The single immediately topped the UK iTunes chart and made its debut at Number 6 in the UK singles chart. A second video 'The Stars (Are Out Tonight)' came in February in which actress

Tilda Swinton played the singer's lover.

Reviews were uniformly ecstatic with the *New York Times* proclaiming it "Mr Bowie's twilight masterpiece" and the *Los Angeles Times* called it "Breath taking, a marvellously successful return". His reappearance in 2013 with new music was welcomed as "the most glorious comeback in pop history" and the London-based *Daily Telegraph* critic gave the album five stars and called it "An absolute wonder – bold, beautiful and baffling".

That same year came a unique event that encapsulated Bowie's long term grip on the imagination of a generation and could be seen as the ultimate tribute to his visionary status. Canadian astronaut Chris Hadfield astounded the beings of Planet Earth by making a video of himself singing David's classic hit 1969 'Space Oddity' actually while on board a real space craft.

As he circled miles overhead on the International Space Station he was filmed singing the now time honoured lyrics that took on even greater meaning.

Singing with due solemnity as befitted a Bowie fan and space rocker, when it came to the magical line, "I'm floating in a most peculiar way…" Hadfield could be seen floating in zero gravity and

Previous pages: On stage at the Verizon Wireless Amphitheater, in Irvine, California, August 13, 2002, on the *Heathen* tour.

Opposite: On his 66th birthday Bowie announced the release of his first single in ten years.

Above: Following the news of Bowie's death, *Blackstar* – released three days earlier – headed to the No.1 spot in many international sales and download charts.

STILL A STARMAN 155

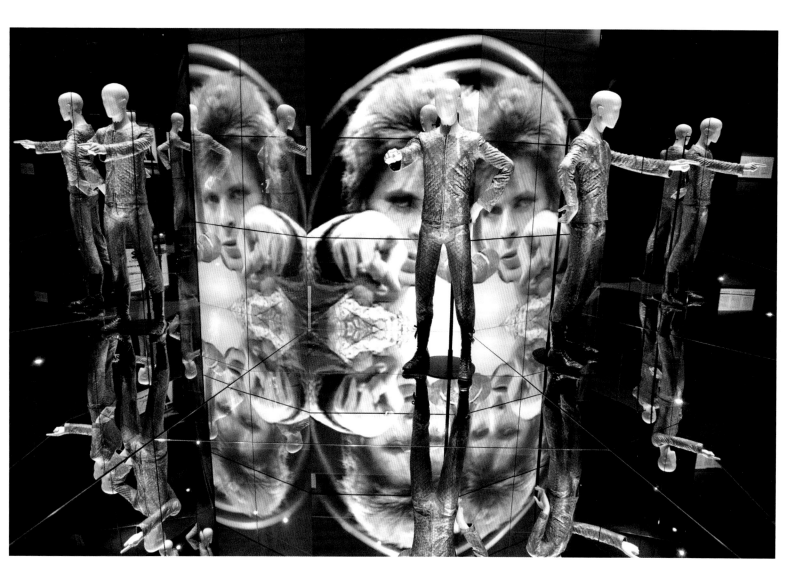

allowing his acoustic guitar to spin around inside the cabin.

It was the first pop video sung and shot in space and was seen by millions on TV and YouTube. This space exploit could be seen as marking a high point in Bowie's prestige as a celebrated internationally admired figure, all the more remarkable given that when the original record was first released (the same year Neil Armstrong took his "giant leap", it was regarded with some distaste and suspicion in NASA circles.

There was still some residual hostility towards him when an exhibition of Bowie artefacts including his stage costumes was staged at London's Victoria and Albert Museum in 2013. At least one art critic felt that it was more of a stunt by the museum than a true cultural event, in an attempt to seek publicity and attract younger, less serious visitors. Whatever the case, it was a huge success. The exhibition, called 'David Bowie Is', later

began a world tour, moving to Toronto and on to Chicago, Paris, Melbourne and finally Groningen in the Netherlands.

Bowie and his family took a far less dramatic but nonetheless satisfying trip, not to the stars, but to London in 2014. It was a homecoming conducted in private. They flew to Luton airport snuck into the UK and the press had no idea about their visit. David took daughter Alexandria, then aged 15 and wife Iman sight-seeing and they visited the places where he grew up. First they went to the Tower of London, walking unnoticed through the crowds. David later went for a trip on the London Eye. Then his driver took him to visit Brixton and the house where he was born David Jones in Stansfield Road.

They went on to Plaistow Grove in Bromley, where his family moved when David was aged six and thence to Foxgrove Road, Beckenham, where he lived in March 1969 and famously sang at the Three Tuns pub in the town's high street. Iman recalled later that they took Alexandria to the house where he had grown up for a family photograph.

Also in 2014 Bowie became the oldest recipient of a Brit Award, winning Best British Male, collected on his behalf by Kate Moss. She read out his speech which said: "I'm delighted to have a Brit

for being best male. But I am, aren't I Kate?|"

In November a compilation album *Nothing Has Changed* was released, including rare tracks and older material, but there was a new single 'Sue (Or in a Season of Crime).' Then December 2015 saw the premiere of David's new stage musical *Lazarus* co-written with Enda Walsh and performed by the New York Theatre Workshop.

It was inspired by the 1963 novel *The Man Who Fell To Earth* that was later made into a movie, starring Bowie as main character Thomas Jerome Newton. *Lazarus* featured 18 new Bowie songs, performed by a band onstage in a striking performance directed by Ivo Van Hove.

Ivo would witness how David was suffering from his terminal illness and sadly saw him collapse with exhaustion at the premiere. He told reporters: "Sometimes I would look at him and I'd be silent for a moment and I'd see tears. Not in his eyes – directly behind his eyes. He was truly suffering, because he did not want to die…"

In the wake of his death there was a surge of interest in Bowie's back catalogue sparked by the success of *Blackstar*. An ecstatic record industry proclaimed that Bowie had made "chart history" as 14 albums and nine singles appeared in the Official Charts in January 2016. They included *The Rise and Fall of Ziggy Stardust And*

The Spiders From Mars. *Hunky Dory* and *Aladdin Sane*, showing the continuing relevance of his work 40 years after David had enjoyed his first hit records.

As tributes from fellow artists poured in Mick Jagger described him as "an inspiration" and fellow Rolling Stone Ronnie Wood said, "We used to have a great laugh with him, because David had a terrific sense of humour".

Blackstar, his 28th album, was described by Tony Visconti as "his parting gift to the fans," continuing on to say: "David always did what he wanted to do. And he wanted to do it his way and do it the best way. His death was no different from his life. It was a work of Art. Although I knew for a year this way the way it would be, I wasn't prepared for it. He was an extraordinary man, full of love and life. He will always be with us. For now it is appropriate to cry."

Above: A moving tribute to Bowie is seen outside the Ritzy cinema in Brixton – the singer's birthplace – on January 11, 2016, following the announcement of his death.

Right: The world's media and thousands of fans gather by a mural of Bowie in Brixton on January 11, 2016 to pay tribute to the singer who had died a day earlier.

PICTURE CREDITS